MODERN CHINESE ARCHITECTURE
180 YEARS

ORO Editions
Publishers of Architecture, Art, and Design
Gordon Goff: Publisher

www.oroeditions.com
info@oroeditions.com

Published by ORO Editions

Author: Nancy Shatzman Steinhardt
Book Design: Pablo Mandel / CircularStudio
Project Manager: Jake Anderson

10 9 8 7 6 5 4 3 2 1 First Edition

ISBN: 978-1-961856-07-3

Prepress and Print work by ORO Editions Inc
Printed in China

ORO Editions makes a continuous effort to minimize the overall carbon footprint of its publications. As part of this goal, ORO, in association with Global ReLeaf, arranges to plant trees to replace those used in the manufacturing of the paper produced for its books. Global ReLeaf is an international campaign run by American Forests, one of the world's oldest nonprofit conservation organizations. Global ReLeaf is American Forests' education and action program that helps individuals, organizations, agencies, and corporations improve the local and global environment by planting and caring for trees.

MODERN CHINESE ARCHITECTURE
180 YEARS

NANCY SHATZMAN STEINHARDT

ORO
EDITIONS

Contents

Preface

In 2020, I was given the opportunity to write the text of a giftbook on the past century of architecture in China. Before then, I had taught buildings of China's twentieth century in lecture courses to undergraduates at the University of Pennsylvania, but my research on this period had been limited to buildings designed by Penn-trained architects following their returns to China. This new engagement with the twentieth and twenty-first centuries gave me the opportunity to grapple with the most-frequently asked question at the end of those undergraduate lectures: What about Chinese architecture today?

I knew I would answer that question with examples of buildings made of reinforced concrete with imitation bracket sets on their facades and ceramic-tile roofs covering them, and made of swirling steel and multilayered glass, and with skyscrapers that competed to be the world's tallest. I knew that art deco and Bauhaus and brutalism had impacted building in China. And I knew the question should be answered not just by famous buildings in Shanghai and other megalopolises, but also by construction from every province. I knew that in contrast to the palaces, temples, ritual altars, and the occasional open-air stage, observatory, guild hall, and academy that were the focuses of research on premodern architecture, the most important architecture of the past century in China would include universities, stadiums, hospitals, museums, train stations, airports, and megamalls. I knew that builders and craftspersons had been replaced by architects whose designs became real through international competitions, that sustainability was inherent in designs of the last several decades, and that the natural materials of premodern vernacular traditions could be adapted to produce sustainable architecture.

Like the giftbook, this one was written during the COVID-19 pandemic, when I was not able to travel to China. Using books, databases, writings by architects, and my own notes, I began where historians of modern China and Chinese architecture have begun for decades: during the First Opium War (1839–1842) when non-Chinese began to build in cities across China. I found nearly 500 buildings worthy of further investigation, sixty-one of which had been discussed in the giftbook.

When I mentioned this research to Penn graduate students in fall 2021, five of them convinced me to hold a seminar on China's modern and contemporary architecture. Bryce Heatherly, Keda Wang, Ran Yan, Kyra Xinwei Yao, Zhu Hao, and I met for three hours a week from January through May of 2022 to study those 500 buildings. Our goal was to select approximately 200 through which modern Chinese architecture was best narrated. Our choices were driven by history, the confirmed or anticipated importance of the structure or its architect, unique or highly unusual features, and always by strong visual impact. Some projects made the final list through eloquent advocacy, and others by vote.

The pages that follow are intended to introduce Chinese architecture of the last 180 years through highly important buildings. As someone who has taught and lectured on Chinese architecture as long as I have, use in the university classroom was central at every stage of writing and image selection. I also hoped this book would be worthwhile reading for residents and travelers in China. I thus have sought illustrations that offer powerful visual impact, for they so often led me to a building in the first place. I include a brief discussion of each building, with the goal that the commentary can be used in the classroom or by the independent reader to provoke longer, deeper, and comparative discussions. I include a modest-sized bibliography, primarily of book-length works.

I organize the material roughly into decades, for I concluded that even if distinctive features are not readily apparent within a ten-year period, enough changed contextually that the rubrics could work. For some decades the selection was much harder than for others; ca. 1910–ca. 1940 and post-2000 were the most challenging periods from which to select. At one point during the last week of class, a student verbalized what had been with us from the beginning: how many of these buildings will be standing or still be important in 100 years? As I made the final selection, that question was with me: Which buildings are most important to know about as period statements in a world in which land is precious and renovation, if not replacement, is likely?

I thank Gordon Goff for his enthusiasm about and confidence in this book from a first, casual conversation through completion. I thank Clare Jacobson, a superb editor who often knew what I was thinking even if I did not explain it clearly enough to be understood. I thank Pablo Mandel for his patience through many versions of layout and editing, and I thank Jake Anderson for managing the process to the most final stage. When it was certain I could not travel in China in 2022–23, Keda Wang offered to make the trip for me. His photographs of more than 100 buildings taken during a four-month period in the spring of 2023 made it possible for this book to be finished. I thank Kyra Xinwei Yao for gathering images of buildings that could not be photographed. Finally I thank Sarah Brooker for proofreading the final version.

中国地图

审图号：GS(2019)1670号 自然资源部 监制

Introduction

CHINESE ARCHITECTURE BECOMES MODERN

In the 180 years from 1840 to 2020, China transformed from a dynasty ruled by emperors to a people's republic, from a country in which fewer than half the male population and perhaps 10 percent of the female population could read to a reported 97 percent literacy, from a nation with a per capita annual income of roughly 500 dollars to more than ten times (by some estimates more than sixty times) that amount, and from a place with a population that was more than 95 percent rural to one that is more than 60 percent urban. In 2022, Chinese architecture served a population of more than 1.45 billion whose gross domestic product had been around $US 16,700 billion in 2021.

Until 1840, the emperor's palace was impenetrable to all but China's imperial elite. Almost every city retained walls or parts of walls from one or more previous centuries. Every city, town, village, and hamlet had Daoist temples and Buddhist monasteries, some with pagodas rising above the primarily single-story buildings, shrines to popular gods, and sometimes a temple to Confucius. Those who could afford them constructed gardens adjacent to their residences. Diversity in traditional building was apparent only in residential architecture outside China's major cities. Otherwise, modular timber-frames—pillars lodged into bases and supporting ceramic-tile roofs, bracket sets joined to beams and pillars, positioned along axial lines and around courtyards, always parts of complexes as opposed to standing alone, and usually marked by front gates—dominated cities and countryside alike.

Between 1840 and 2020, China witnessed the transformation from single-story structures to buildings that soared 100 stories above ground alongside temple markets, peddlers, and megamalls. Open-air stages for local audiences were supplanted by auditoriums and stadiums with cutting-edge acoustics for tens of thousands. Civic architecture, public parks, and green spaces replaced imperial altars and private gardens. Doctors worked in hospitals more often than as village or itinerant practitioners and universities replaced academies. Oxcarts and trains were superseded by travel above and below ground via train, plane, and automobile, and anonymous local builders and craftspeople were replaced by international starchitects.

With modern architecture came new technology, which sometimes resulted in social change. The first elevator, first urban water system, first university accredited in the United States, and first psychiatric hospital were introduced to China between the 1860s and 1890s. China's first park opened in an international settlement in 1868. A telephone exchange and electricity were first seen in 1882, and in 1883 Shanghai Waterworks opened. Cars arrived in Shanghai in 1901, trams in 1908, and the first manned flight in 1911.

The first century of modern architecture in China was a period of warfare: the First Opium War (1839–1842), the Second Opium War (1856–1860), the Taiping Rebellion (1850–1864), the Sino-French War (1883–1885), the Boxer Rebellion (1900–1901), border conflict with Russia in 1895 and 1900, and fighting with Japan in 1904–1905 occurred in rapid succession or simultaneously. Imperial China collapsed in 1911. The next year, Sun Yat-sen (1866–1925) became the provisional president of the Republic of China, but was immediately succeeded by Yuan Shikai (1859–1916), inaugurating a period sometimes described as warlordism. The 1930s brought the Japanese into Manchuria. By the end of the decade, Japan had moved deeper into China, and affiliates of most of China's universities and research institutions had fled to the southwest. Decades of political upheaval followed. Upon the end of World War II, civil war erupted between China's Nationalists and Communists, ending in the establishment of the People's Republic in 1949. Next were campaigns and movements: the Hundred Flowers Campaign began in 1956, and then the Anti-Rightest Campaign in 1957, the Great Leap Forward in 1958, and the Cultural Revolution in 1966, which ended the year Mao Zedong (1893–1976) died. Buildings rose in greater numbers during the economic reform of Chairman Deng Xiaoping (1904–1997) in the 1980s, followed by the unprecedented foreign investment in China beginning in the 1990s under the leadership of Jiang Zemin (1926-2022), then Hu Jintao (b. 1942), and then Xi Jinping (b. 1953).

Although it can be argued that China sought to modernize its architecture in the early twentieth century, the architectural movement known as *modernism* (which is different from a building labeled "modern") was widely apparent across China in the later twentieth century. *Modernism* is a broadly encompassing word that indicates a turn toward the newer, the more technologically advanced, and the innovative. All three occurred in the buildings that are said to express Chinese modernism. These buildings were often made of reinforced concrete, steel, and glass, and they were characterized by an understanding that form should follow function (functionalism), that simplicity and pure geometric forms should supersede decoration (minimalism), and that sometimes the structure itself should be visible in a building (structuralism). By the end of the century, architects knew that with the right technology, a static structure could exhibit motion (futurism), a concept that would be carried to new heights in the twenty-first century.

During these 180 years since 1840, two self-referential frameworks have characterized Chinese architecture, neither of which has complete clarity. Four Chinese words *jindai*, *xiandai*, *dangdai*, and *dangdangdai* are used in the first. I translate *jindai* as modern and understand it as beginning in 1840 and as ending in 1949. I divide this very long period into three parts, and note that some writings about modern Chinese architecture use 1937, the year of the start of war with Japan, as the terminus of *jindai*. *Xiandai*, which I translate as contemporary, follows. It covers the years 1949–1978, from the founding of the People's Republic to the point when, after nearly thirty years of isolation, Chinese students and others began to study and travel in the West again. *Dangdai*, meaning right now, refers to the period after 1978, but its forty-five-year-and-counting duration as well as its large number of extraordinary buildings and architects requires further division. I use the millennium as the divide, so that *dangdai* refers to architecture of 1978–2000, and *dangdai* architects to those who were most productive during that period. *Dangdangdai*—which means right, right now—is the period after 2000. *Dangdangdangdai* is used with a chuckle by architects in recognition that building has been contemporary for many decades and new categorization is in order.

The second set of divisions of the architecture of the past 180 years suggests a relationship between where architects study and the designs they construct. The First Generation of modern Chinese architects is widely accepted as referring to those who studied abroad immediately after World War I. They returned to China to initiate programs in architectural design at universities or to establish firms that built structures of the kind theretofore constructed only by foreigners outside China or in China. It is more difficult to define each successive generation, because the Second Generation and even the Third Generation of modern Chinese architects begin while some of the First Generation are still working. I define Second Generation as beginning in the 1950s, roughly contemporary with *xiandai* architecture. This generation learned the profession almost exclusively in China. The Third Generation is defined as the group who studied abroad or trained in China in the 1980s through around 2000, while architects trained after 2000 are the Fourth Generation. In the discussion that follows, I employ the six chronological divisions.

Early Jindai, 1840–1912

WAR, CONCESSIONS, TREATY PORTS, BANKS, UNIVERSITIES, CHURCHES

By the early nineteenth century, British ships were bringing opium into China despite the Chinese prohibition against its sale. This was a full 200 years after John Watts (1550–1616) founded the East India Company, on December 31, 1600, with the goal of controlling trade between England, South Asia, and Southeast Asia, and later, East Asia. Before and after 1600, with a few exceptions, Portuguese attempts to trade in China were largely unsuccessful beyond Macau. By the end of the seventeenth century, Dutch traders were docking at ports in Southeast China and trading with Japan. George Macartney's (1737–1806) meeting with the Qianlong emperor (r. 1736–1795) in Chengde in 1793 failed to garner the desired British trading privileges in China. Rights at Chinese ports came to a head in 1839 when China attempted to limit and control the amount of opium entering on British ships. The end of the First Opium War, officially marked by the signing of the Treaty of Nanking in 1842, resulted in the opening of five treaty ports—Guangzhou (formerly Canton), Xiamen (formerly Amoy), Fuzhou (formerly Foochow), Ningbo (formerly Ningpo), and Shanghai—and the cession of Hong Kong to England. By the end of 1843, eleven foreign mercantile institutions were in Shanghai.

Much of the architecture in foreign-friendly ports was built along the waterfront, known as the Bund. The Chinese word for this area is *waitan*, meaning outer beach or waterfront. The name bund most often is associated with the 1.5-kilometer stretch of fifty-two buildings that runs along the west side of the Huangpu River in Shanghai. Bund also is used to refer to waterfront architecture of European design at major treaty ports such as Hankou (part of Wuhan). The waterfront locations were opportunities for architects, most of whom were foreign in the early Jindai period, to showcase buildings that offered China her first public views of modernism. Prior to this, modern buildings had been commissioned solely by Chinese emperors for their private enjoyment. Outside treaty ports, secular and Chinese religious construction continued according to millennial-old patterns.

Roman Catholicism had entered China in the Tang dynasty (618–917). Missionaries had built churches in Beijing, Yangzhou, and Quanzhou during the period of Mongolian rule in the thirteenth and fourteenth centuries. The Jesuit Matteo Ricci (1552–1610) established a mission in China in 1601, followed by a steady stream of Jesuits and then Augustinians, Dominicans, and Franciscans. The facade of St. Paul's Cathedral in Macau, built from 1602–1640, is often considered the oldest extant church architecture in China, with St. Paul's in Melaka, consecrated in 1521, understood as a predecessor. An imperial edict of 1844 stated that Chinese would not be punished for becoming Christian, and two years later the Daoguang emperor (r. 1821–1850) permitted missionaries to reclaim buildings that had been used by them in the past. Probably not coincidentally, the oldest complete churches standing in China date from the 1840s. Like Roman Catholicism, Protestantism came first to Macau and its first churches were in China's five treaty ports.

The opportunities for foreign architects were greater in China than many of the places from which they came. Some came to China specifically for the chance to design new buildings, but others, who came for adventure or as refugees, understood the opportunities for construction only when they began to practice. Many of their creations would be of unprecedented scale and permanence on the Chinese landscape.

THE 1840s

The 1840s was the third and final decade of rule by the Daoguang emperor. He was ineffective in squelching the sale of opium, for which he blamed his minister Lin Zexu (1785–1850). European-style architecture rose in the treaty ports during this decade, and European commercial construction continued on islands and in ports such as Macau and Haikou. Building by imperial commission and by and for China's wealthiest population remained as it had been before non-Chinese architecture appeared in China.

THE 1850s

Warfare continued in the 1850s. Between 1850 and 1864, a Christian uprising against the Qing dynasty (1644–1912) government known as the Taiping Rebellion raged from Nanjing southward. In 1856, the British attacked Guangzhou and Tianjin, initiating the Second Opium War. France, Russia, and the United States joined the British Empire in fighting China. In Beijing, French and British forces burned the Summer Palace (Yiheyuan) and the so-called European Mansions, stone structures designed by Europeans for the imperial garden Yuanmingyuan. The Treaty of Tientsin (today Tianjin)—signed in 1858 with the United States, England, France, and Russia—opened eleven more treaty ports and brought additional foreign legations to Beijing.

THE 1860s

In 1860, China signed a treaty with Russia, formally establishing a border that placed the maritime region of Vladivostok in Russian hands. In 1861 the throne of China passed from the Xianfeng emperor (r. 1851–1861) to his five-year-old son, who became the Tongzhi emperor (r. 1862–1874). Power passed to his mother, the empress dowager Cixi (1835–1908), and the less influential empress dowager Ci'an (1837–1881). By the end of the decade, the Japanese emperor Meiji (r. 1868–1912) assumed nominal power, and Japan was on its way to modernization. Political and social reforms in Japan would impact modernization in China for the next eighty years. By the 1860s, European architecture had a twenty-year history in China, and architectural styles of European countries were apparent.

THE 1870s

The decade begins with the Tianjin Massacre in June of 1870, incited by rumors that French Sisters of Charity were killing Chinese children. The French consul was among sixty people killed in front of Wanghailou Church, which was destroyed. China's apology to France probably prevented an immediate war. Tongzhi's successor, the Guangxu emperor (r. 1875–1908), ascended the throne in 1875, at an age even younger than his predecessor. The Summer Palace, where Cixi spent much of her time, was rebuilt during this period. The most important modern architecture that survives from this decade is in Tianjin and Shanghai.

THE 1880s

This was another decade of treaties and war. In 1881, China and Russia signed the Treaty of St. Petersburg to clarify China's northwestern border. China emerged victorious from the Tonkin War with France, fought for less than a year in 1884–1885. Although China fared better than in some earlier wars of the century, it signed a peace treaty in Tianjin giving control of Annam and Tonkin (Vietnam) to France. In 1887, China signed the Treaty of Peking, recognizing Macau as Portuguese. Important new construction in China was still designed in traditional styles. Yet the first urban water system in China opened in Shanghai during this decade.

THE 1890s

In 1898 at the age of twenty-seven, the Guangxu emperor enacted a series of ambitious reforms aimed at modernizing China. Kang Youwei (1858–1927) and Liang Qichao (1873–1929) inspired and guided him. Less than a year later, Guangxu promulgated broad-based educational, political, economic, and social reforms. They became known as the Hundred Days of Reform because they were extinguished before the end of the year. Guangxu spent the remainder of his life under house arrest, power returning to Cixi. The dowager died a day later than he, his death probably the result of poisoning.

The First Sino-Japanese War occurred in 1894–1895, ending with Korea's independence from China, and China paying Japan for the return of the Liaodong Peninsula. In 1898, Russia leased Dalian, including Port Arthur, from China, France leased Guangzhou Island, and Britain leased Port Edward and the city Weihai in Shandong province as well as Hong Kong and the adjacent New Territories.

By the 1890s, eclecticism was present in Chinese architecture. A movement that began in Europe, the style quickly spread west to North America and east across Asia. Eclectic buildings were often large, bold, and symmetrical and had highly decorated surfaces that referenced architecture from distant places. European-style works that referenced ancient Greece and Rome and the Italian Renaissance exhibited eclecticism in China. Construction of the Trans-Siberian Railway began in 1891. The population of China at this time was about 450 million.

THE 1900s

Cathedrals, schools, offices, factories, Western-style housing, and consulates in brick, stone, and reinforced concrete stood in every Chinese city that had a foreign presence in the 1900s. Their architects were European, American, and Japanese. Imperial construction, residences of the wealthy, and houses of Chinese religions continued to be built according to architectural principles that had been in place for centuries. It would take one more war and, most importantly, education to transform society and turn Chinese architecture modern.

That war was the Boxer Rebellion, begun by villagers in 1900 but supported by the Qing government. At that time China also was fighting Russia at Blagoveshchensk and the Sixty-Four Villages near the Amur River. In 1903, Sir Francis Younghusband led a British expedition to Tibet, bringing about the opening of two treaty ports in 1904. The border between China and Korea was established in 1909. Through sixty years of struggle, political reform, and the modernization that was integral to it had not been achieved.

At the turn of the century, it became popular for architects to design buildings entered on the corner that they expanded to either side of cross streets. Several of China's most forward-looking construction projects, such as waterworks, began during this decade. Other ongoing building projects came to crashing halts with the fall of the Qing dynasty.

Architect unknown, Thirteen Factories

Guangzhou
1842

In the late seventeenth century, China permitted trade with Holland and England during set periods at a few ports, one of which was Guangzhou, then known as Canton. A superintendent of customs strictly controlled trade, and foreigners had to leave Canton, usually for Macau, when the trading season ended. While in residence in Canton, the Europeans lived in buildings called *factories*, a name derived from the English word *factor* meaning commercial agent.

These factories, known as *hong* in Chinese, included shops as well as warehouses and living quarters. American, Austrian, British, Danish, Dutch, French, Spanish, and Swedish traders lived in two- or three-story buildings with European facades. They were arranged around courtyards and had rooms on either side of long, narrow arcades. The factories, built as early as 1757, were rebuilt after fires in 1822 and 1841, the second a result of the First Opium War. In 1856, Guangzhou's foreign settlement left the factories and moved to Shamian Island, and the factories were abandoned. The factories are sometimes compared to architecture on the artificial island Dejima, in Nagasaki, Japan, settled by the Portuguese in 1634.

Architect unknown, Shopping Arcade

Haikou
1849

Haikou on Hainan Island is known for *qilou*, structures of two or more stories with shopping arcades fronted by verandas on the first floor and residences above. The oldest arcades date to 1849, and most of the remaining buildings date to the early 1900s. They comprise the largest extant century-old shopping arcade in China, more than 600 buildings along more than thirty streets in an area of about 25,000 square meters. Many of the buildings were constructed by émigrés to Hainan from treaty ports as well as other parts of South China and Southeast Asia.

邂逅民宿
Meet B & B
20

Thomaz de Aquino, Governor's Residence

Macau
1849

Today a state guest house known as Government House and before 1999 the residence of the governor of Macau, this estate was built by the local architect Thomaz de Aquino in Pombaline style. The architectural style was named after the marquess de Pombal, Sebastião de Carvalho (1699–1782), who led the rebuilding of Lisbon in the aftermath of the great earthquake of 1755. With a goal of earthquake resistance, Pombaline buildings are rarely more than four stories and are supported by a wooden frame that, like the Chinese timber frame, offers a certain amount of resistance to shaking.
In Portuguese cities, the Pombaline use of first-floor arcades for shops, placement of buildings along orthogonal lines, and design of repetitive windows with minimal decoration signaled a modesty of expenditure in line with the goal of urban renewal. Macau had become a Portuguese colony in 1557 and remained one until 1887.

Architect unknown, Vernacular Architecture

Hongcun
mid-nineteenth century

During the mid-nineteenth century, residential architecture in China's countryside continued to follow age-old patterns, to self-identify by its region and local population, and to be restored according to early construction styles long after governmental, educational, and medical architecture changed in response to technological innovations and social needs. Architecture in and around Hongcun, a village in the Huizhou region of Anhui province, is representative of its region. Other identifiable vernacular traditions are Beijing *hutong*, Tibetan blockhouses, circular or elliptical compounds of the Kejia (Hakka) people in Guangdong, earth-sheltered dwellings in North China, residences raised on stilts in the south, and drum towers in Guizhou.

White-washed exterior walls, flat facades that taper towards the top known as *matouqiang* (horse-head walls), dark tile roofs, prominent and decorated entryways, and intricate carving in stone, brick, and wood characterize Hongcun vernacular architecture. Rooms are usually two and occasionally three stories and are built around courtyards. Lightwells are common in Hongcun's vernacular buildings.

Father Nicholas Massa, St. Francis Xavier Cathedral

Shanghai
1853

Located near the small French Concession in Shanghai, this cathedral was built as a replacement for a Catholic church erected in Shanghai in 1553 that had been turned into a temple to the Chinese war god Guandi. It was done in neo-baroque style inspired by the design of St. Ignatius of Loyola Church in Rome.

Architect unknown, Astor House Hotel

Shanghai
1858 and later

By the mid 1850s, the majority of foreign architecture—mercantile buildings, shops, residences, a hotel, and a club in Shanghai—was on the Bund, the embankment along the west side of the Huangpu River, a tributary of the Yangzi River, where much of Shanghai's and China's most important real estate would rise in the 1920s and 1930s. Astor House Hotel was relocated there in 1857. In 1844, the Scottish sea merchant Peter Felix Richards (1808–1868), one of the first foreigners to work in Shanghai, built a hotel and restaurant of this name that served Western food. In 1857 the hotel was relocated under new ownership.

The 1876 version of Astor House Hotel comprised four neo-Renaissance buildings linked together by passageways. In 1881 it was the first building in China with electric lights, and two years later it was the first building in Shanghai with running water. The first motion picture in Shanghai was shown there in 1897. Management changed hands every few years from the late nineteenth century on, but the hotel maintained premier and then acquired historic status not just in China but internationally. In the 1930s, however, it vied for premier status in Shanghai with the Cathay Hotel. Renovation of the Astor House Hotel in neo-baroque style was completed in 1910, at which time the building had twenty-four-hour hot water and a telephone in every room. From 1920 to 1949, the Shanghai Stock Exchange was located here. The ballroom was renovated in 1923. In 1937, the hotel was occupied by the Japanese. After the war with Japan, it returned to private Chinese control, then was owned by the Shanghai Land and Housing Bureau, and then became part of the Shanghai Institution Business Administrative Bureau. It became Pujiang Hotel in 1959, and after that, a youth hostel. The hotel was extensively renovated in 2006.

浦江飯店
中国证券博物馆

Architect unknown, Dingling, Tomb of the Xianfeng Emperor

Zunhua
1861

The tombs of emperors of the Qing dynasty who ruled from Beijing divide into two groups. The eastern group is a complex of eighty square kilometers in Zunhua, Hebei province, 125 kilometers northeast of Beijing, and the western group occupies about 100 square kilometers in Yi County, 120 kilometers south of Beijing. Five emperors are interred in the eastern group and four are in the west, with wives, concubines, and other relatives in each group. Dingling is in the eastern group, among about 300 buildings that comprise the tombs of fifteen empresses, 136 concubines, a prince, and four other emperors.

The Dingling Tomb and the ancillary cemetery around it follow patterns of Chinese imperial funerary design that trace to the Han dynasty (202 BCE–220 CE), with the greatest resemblance to tombs of the Ming dynasty. Like the thirteen Ming tombs north of Beijing, the eastern Qing royal cemetery begins at a freestanding ceremonial archway. This is followed by a single-story, red gate set in an outer wall to its east and west. Next is a pavilion with a freestanding column at each corner; this covers a tortoise base supporting a stele inscribed with the meritorious deeds of the first emperor buried in the complex. Pairs of standing and kneeling animals, statues of civil and military officials, a glazed screen wall with three openings, and the stele pavilion and halls for the founding emperor are next.

Xianfeng's own tomb, the farthest west of the imperial tombs, repeats in small-scale the layout of the tomb of the earliest emperor buried in the royal cemetery. A shorter path lined with statues, a five-entry ceremonial gate, a stele pavilion, bridges over water, and a gate opening into a wall-enclosed courtyard containing a hall for sacrifices lead to a final pavilion and the burial mound.

Architect unknown, Astor Hotel

Tianjin
1864

The Astor Hotel was begun in 1863 and completed the next year under the direction of the British Methodist missionary John Innocent (1829–1904). The Sino-Denmark Treaty and the Sino-Netherlands Treaty were signed at Astor Hotel in its first year. By 1884 the hotel was a three-story structure—the tallest building in the British Concession.

In 1924 a second building was added to it and Otis Company installed a passenger elevator. Astor Hotel's fourth story was added in 1929. Presidents Ulysses S. Grant (1822–1885) and Herbert Hoover (1874–1964) stayed there, the latter during the Boxer Rebellion. The hotel was renovated in 2010.

Architect unknown, Chartered Bank of India, Australia, and China

Hankou
1865

Hankou (Hankow) was not one of China's first five treaty ports. Rather, it became important in the early 1860s following the Treaty of Tientsin. The location, far up the Yangzi River, made it the take-off point for commerce in north central China, much of it along the Han River that joined the Yangzi. In 1850 Hankou had an estimated population of 1 million. It is natural that the Chartered Bank of India, Australia, and China, vested in 1853 with the goal of becoming one of the greatest British colonial banks, had a branch here. It opened as the first Western bank in the city in 1863. The bank and British Concession were on a street behind the Bund, making it less likely to be flooded by the Yangzi River. Chartered Bank of India, Australia, and China had opened for business in Shanghai in 1858, the same year it opened in Kolkata (Calcutta) and Mumbai (Bombay).

The eighth Lord Elgin (Thomas Bruce Elgin [1811–1863]), son of the seventh (Lord Thomas Bruce Elgin [1766–1841], who had overseen the removal of marbles from the Parthenon), ordered the destruction of the Western Mansions at the imperial garden Yuanmingyuan and was present when the Treaty of Tientsin was signed, recognized the potential importance of the location of Hankou before it became a treaty port. In 1861, the diplomat Sir Robert Hart (1835–1911), who would live in China for fifty-four years, opened the port. There were forty foreigners in Hankou at that time. Hankou retains several of the most important buildings in China designed by Europeans in the 1860s. It was the commercial center among the cities that comprise the metropolis of Wuhan today.

湘味小炒

Sir George Gilbert Scott and William Kidner, Holy Trinity Church

Shanghai
1869

Holy Trinity Church is a rare example of Christian architecture built in China in the 1860s that has survived in close to its original form through more than 150 years of political change. Land for the first church on this site was purchased by British working in Shanghai in 1847. That structure collapsed three years later. Subsequently Sir George Gilbert Scott (1811–1878), a British architect known for British Gothic Revival construction, was hired to design the church. Scott counts Midland Grant Hotel at St. Pancras Station, King's College Chapel, and Albert Memorial in Hyde Park, all in London, and the main building of the University as well as St. Mary's Cathedral, in Glasgow, among his designs. Scott's name is associated with more than 800 buildings. He never traveled to Shanghai, but rather drew a design with a nave, two transepts, two aisles, and a chancel for the church. William Kidner (1841–1900) of Scott's firm saw the design to completion, making changes to fit the budget and growing number of foreigners in Shanghai. A spire added in 1901 was destroyed during the Cultural Revolution. Zhang Ming Architectural Design restored the church in the twenty-first century.

Architect unknown, Wanghailou Church

Tianjin
1870

Wanghai Tower (*lou*) was built on this site during the reign of the Kangxi emperor (r. 1662–1722) for imperial visits. Wanghailou Church, also known as Notre Dame des Victoires, replaced it in 1870 as the first Catholic church in Tianjin. Located outside the concessions, it was the site of the Tianjin Massacre the following year. Rebuilt in 1897, it would burn again during the Boxer Rebellion in 1900, be rebuilt for the last time in 1904, and be renovated after a major earthquake struck Tianjin in 1976. Still, today it is largely unchanged from its original appearance.

Wanghailou Church is sixteen meters across the front and fifty-five meters deep. The two-story, brick structure has a twelve-meter tower at the central front with shorter, corner towers. All three are bell towers. The domed apse, a nave, shorter side aisles, and pointed-arched windows in the front and sides, as well as on the towers, define the structure as Gothic. The interior space is ten-by-thirty meters. The small, octagonal towers at the four corners of the chapel were not part of the original design. The animal heads on them that serve for drainage may follow Chinese architectural precedents.

N.D. DES VICTOIRES

Architect unknown, Society for the Study of Chinese Architecture Site

Yibin
1874

Built in 1874 as the residence of a family named Zhang, Liang Sicheng (1901–1971), Lin Huiyin (1904-1955), and other members of the Society for the Study of Chinese Architecture (Zhongguo Yingzao Xueshe) used this courtyard-style compound for their research institute as well as residence when they relocated to China's southwest in the late 1930s during the war with Japan. Working in close, humble quarters, Liang, Lin, and Liu Dunzhen (1897–1968), who relocated there from Nanjing, trained some of China's most outstanding architects and architectural history students, including Mo Zongjiang (1916–1999) and Luo Zhewen (1924–2012), during the years when northern and eastern universities such as Tsinghua and Nanjing were closed.

Although restored in the twenty-first century, the buildings retain late-nineteenth-century woodworking and features that identify *chuandou* (column-and-beam) construction, a form used primarily in vernacular buildings that produces flat walls and overhanging eaves. Today the buildings house a museum about the Society and its major discoveries.

Architect unknown, Hu Xueyan Mansion

Hangzhou
1875

Hu Xueyan (1823–1885), one of China's most successful merchants in the 1870s and early 1880s, was born to a poor family in Anhui province. He rose to become the owner of his own bank, financial firm, and pawnshops. He also dealt in arms, silk, and medicinal goods. In 1875, the dowager Cixi gave Hu an official title and put him in charge of the financial and civil administration of Hangzhou. But eight years later his business collapsed, and he lost his official position.

The Hu Xueyan Mansion spans 5,815 square meters. It cost, according to some estimates, 3 million taels of silver to construct. The residence is laid out as a traditional Chinese building complex with the four most important buildings along an axial line, courtyards of subsidiary buildings for Hu's wives to their right, and a garden on their left. The buildings use expensive woods such as ginkgo, rosewood, sandalwood, fir, and beech for the timber frame, decorative panels, and furniture. The garden has maze-like passages, formed by a bridge, water, rock, and lighting that renders dark and light spaces of the kind known to have existed in private residential architecture at least since the Ming dynasty. The largest human-made karst grotto in China is beneath the garden. Although the design exhibits so much of Chinese construction, in business Hu was known for employing Westerners and using machinery found in Western companies.

Architect unknown, Shi Family Mansion

Tianjin
1875

The residence and business center of Shi Yuanshi in the Xiqing district of Tianjin comprises more than 200 structures that occupy more than 6,000 square meters. The mansion follows the traditional arrangement of a prominent family, with main courtyards, in this case four, along an axis and additional courtyards of buildings on the eastern and western sides.

The three courtyards on the east were used as residences for the Shi family. A Buddha hall and the largest private theater in China were on the west, and the business office was in the north. Servants' quarters were on the two sides. A garden of 1,200 square meters was added in the early twenty-first century. Today the compound includes a museum of folk art.

小心台阶
小心地滑

Architect unknown, Yuantongbao Hall and Gude Buddhist Monastery

Hankou
1877

Gude Buddhist Monastery is unique in China: it uses a blend of South and Southeast Asian architectural styles with elements of Islamic, Christian, and Greek architecture. Founded by a Buddhist monk, with additions through the 1920s, the site was destroyed by flood in 1931 and rebuilt by 1944. Occupying 8,000 square meters, Yuantongbao Hall is the monastery's main structure.

Yuantongbao Hall houses twenty-five statues of bodhisattvas. Its corner towers follow buildings in Southeast Asia, crucifixes project above them, pointed arches and rose windows reference Christian architecture, scalloped archways point to India and Islam, multiarmed deities of Brahmanism stand alongside Christian imagery, and a floral motif, rather than a European crest, appears above the entry.

Architect unknown, Post Office

Tianjin
1878

In 1878, the German-born British officer Gustav Detring (1842–1913) of the Tianjin Customs Taxation Department founded the Tianjin Customs Correspondence Hall. This was the beginning of Qing China's first post office, built the same year. China's first stamps, *dalong* (great dragon), were issued there in 1878, twelve years after the Qing court had ordered the production of Chinese stamps. (Before then, foreign countries had controlled their own flow of mail in and out of China.) Initially mail with Chinese stamps was carried between Beijing, Tianjin, and Shanghai, and most of it was delivered to and from foreigners in the concessions. The two-story Post Office of brick and wood combines European neoclassicism, as seen in the archways above its windows, and Chinese decorative carving in brick. Today the building is a postal museum.

William Halsey Wood, St. John's University

Shanghai
1879

St. John's College was founded in 1879 by the Episcopal Bishop Joseph Schereschewsky (1831–1906). Newark, New Jersey–based architect William Halsey Wood (1855–1897) designed the initial courtyard. An Anglican who had studied in England, Wood designed primarily Anglican architecture and residences in the style of Henry Hobson Richardson (1838–1886).

In 1891, English became the main language of instruction at St. John's. Three years later, Shanghai-based architect Brenan Atkinson (1866–1907) was hired to design a new main building named Schereschewsky Hall. St. John's quickly became a premier university in China.

In 1905 it was registered in the United States, a distinction that allowed its graduates to apply to graduate and professional schools in America. In 1907, it was the first Chinese university to grant the Bachelor of Arts degree. John Dewey visited in 1919. Like all institutions in Shanghai, St. John's suffered during the Sino-Japanese War. It resumed operations in 1940, but in 1952 most of the university became part of East China Normal and Fudan universities. The campus later became East China University of Political Science and Law.

For the thirty years leading up to the establishment of St. John's, foreign architects had seized on the extraordinary opportunity of designing buildings that were unique on China's landscape. Universities offered this on an expansive scale. The late-nineteenth-century buildings of St. John's University are early evidence of a new kind of building that would stand throughout China, a kind that would combine Western and Chinese architecture. At St. John's, buildings of brick with Western heating and plumbing were covered with Chinese-inspired ceramic-tile roofs with clear ridges at the top and corners and eaves that sloped gracefully upward. These "big hats," as the roofs were nicknamed, would dominate Chinese universities and public buildings through the 1950s. Robert (Wenzhou) Fan (1893-1979) studied engineering here before coming to the University of Pennsylvania to study architecture.

Gabriel James Morrison, Russell & Company Building

Shanghai
1881

Russell & Company was the largest and one of the oldest US trading companies in China. In 1818, Samuel Wadsworth Russell (1789–1862) signed a five-year contract with three other merchants to take charge of a Guangzhou-based firm that would become Russell & Company. From 1830, when Russell left the company, until 1891, when it dissolved, Russell & Company was the most successful American company in China.

Russell & Company had offices in Guangzhou as well as Shanghai. In Shanghai, it occupied a building on the Bund beginning in the 1840s. In 1881 its four-story Shanghai office, today one of the oldest buildings on the Bund, was designed in Victorian neo-Gothic style by Gabriel James Morrison (1840–1905). Born in London, Morrison won three prizes during his engineering studies in Glasgow. He supervised the installation of telegraph cables and railroads, then took a job as chief engineer for one of the major railway lines in China. Upon leaving that work in 1876, Morrison established a civil engineering practice in Shanghai and eventually became the president of the Shanghai Society of Engineers and Architects. In 1885, Morrison partnered with Frederick M. Gratton (1859–1918), a fellow of the Royal Institute of British Architects who had come to China in 1882, to form the architecture and engineering firm Morrison and Gratton.

Architect unknown, Jade Buddha Temple

Shanghai
1882

The Jade Buddha Temple was founded in 1882 to house two white jade Buddhas. One, two meters in height, is in the seated pose of the Buddha at the moment of enlightenment; the other, one meter tall, reclines on its side in a position known as *parinirvana*, which represents the death of the historical Buddha Shakyamuni. The statues were two of the five given to Huigen, a monk of the Chan (meditational) sect, by the king of Myanmar (Burma). During China's 1911 Revolution, the statues were moved out for safe storage. They were returned in 1928, after a new structure was built for statuary. A four-meter-long *parinirvana* statue was brought to the monastery from Singapore in 1989.

The monastery is an example of the continued use and repair of traditional-style temple architecture of Chinese Buddhism in the late nineteenth and early twentieth centuries. Beyond the entry gate, the Hall of Divine Kings houses the guardian deities of the four world quarters. To the right is the Mahavira Hall, where Buddhas of the past, present, and future are enthroned with monks on either side of them and the bodhisattva Guanyin behind them. Behind Mahavira Hall is the tall Jade Buddha Tower that holds the seated jade Buddha and more than 7,000 Buddhist scriptures. The four-meter Buddha in *parinirvana* pose is in its own hall behind these front courtyards.

慈航普渡
苦海津梁

John William Hart, Yangshupu Waterworks

Shanghai
1883

In the 1860s, increasing concerns were raised about impurities in China's water system, especially in cities. Uses of water for laundries and restaurants as well as public health issues concerning water came to the fore. Attempts to right this situation failed until the 1880s, when London-educated attorney Robert E. Wainewright (d. 1892) became involved in the project. He would oversee all legal matters relevant to Shanghai's first modernized water system. Construction began under chief engineer John William Hart (1836–1900). A meeting between Wainewright, Hart, and the powerful Qing official Li Hongzhang (1823–1892) in 1883 underscored the importance of a widespread, sanitary water supply to China. Li opened the first valve at Yangshupu that year. Soon after, Tianjin, Hankou, and Guangzhou had their own waterworks.

Yangshupu Waterworks is the source of four major water lines. Small towers stand at the entrance, and imitation crenellations are above the two-story building of gray brick with red trim. The castle-like structure continues in many buildings across the thirty-two-acre site, which doubled to sixty-four acres by the 1930s.

830

Architect unknown, Xiheying Church

Zhangjiakou
1887

The church in Xiheying village, northwest of Beijing in Hebei province, served a humble, rural congregation of about 500 local Catholics and was a hub for more than 2,000 parishioners of other churches in other towns. It is a rare church that survived the Boxer Rebellion, although 117 of its constituents died in the uprising. Xiheying had maintained a Catholic presence since the 1860s. A chapel had been built there in 1871, and a convent came ten years later. Oriented southward, Xiheying Church stands inside a courtyard, like any major Chinese building. The church is made of simple, gray brick. Still, the front facade has a rose window above a high, central section and four pillars capped with spires, the two central pillars higher and all four extending beyond the roof line. The ground plan is rectangular, and a nave runs from the entrance to the altar at the back.

Alphonse Frédéric de Moerloose and others, Church of the Savior

Beijing
1890

The Church of the Savior, also known as Xishiku and Beitang, is the northern of four major Catholic churches in Beijing. It was founded on land near the Forbidden City granted by the Kangxi emperor in appreciation of Jesuits who had helped him recover from an illness. Completed in 1703, closed in 1827, and reopened after the Second Opium War, it was moved to its present site farther west in 1890 when the empress dowager Cixi decided to appropriate its original site for herself. Lazarist Bishop Pierre-Marie-Alphonse Favier (1837–1905) raised money for construction. (His residence was in a side courtyard.) Favier also led the defense of more than 3,000 Chinese Catholics who took refuge in the church during Boxer attacks. It was the only Beijing church that survived the incursions.

The tripartite front facade has a rose window in the center and two tall turrets, each with two rows of lancet windows, flanking the central portion. The tall, narrow presentation was an attempt at Gothic Revival, inspired by Augustus Pugin's (1762–1832) anti-modernist promotion of a return to construction principles of earlier periods. Upon the church's completion, court officials came to Favier to protest the exaggerated height of the building in its Chinese context. Still, the front courtyard, lions in front of the stairs, lions that cap the white marble balustrade, the balustrade itself, and the Chinese pavilions with two sets of roof eaves place the church in Chinese space.

Aspects of the history of the Catholic Church in China since the Tang dynasty are narrated on stained-glass windows inside.

Architect unknown,
Gate of Supreme Harmony, Forbidden City

Beijing
1894

Forbidden City refers to the walled city inside a walled city inside a walled city, adjacent to a walled city. Today it is at the heart of a city of more than 22 million people. With a majority of buildings supported by timber frames, rotting and repair are inevitable. Even as modern architecture rose in China, the Forbidden City, rightly described as China's ultimate achievement in architecture and one of the most important building complexes on Earth, continued to receive attention. Part of the significance of the Forbidden City is that it has withstood internal change and all that occurred outside its walls through the course of the Ming (1368–1644) and Qing (1644-1912) dynasties and in the subsequent century. Another powerful feature of the architecture is that, exemplary of Chinese construction, individual building components and even entire structures can be replaced according to the underlying modular system.

The Gate of Supreme Harmony burned to the ground in 1886. Rebuilding was completed six years later.

Supreme Harmony is the second of five gates along the main building line of imperial Beijing. It is behind Meridian (Wu) Gate, the entrance to the imperial space, and it marks the entrance to the governing courtyard, the second of three courtyards along the same south-north line. It stands as it has since the early fifteenth century when the emperor held morning court there. The massive gate occupies 1,371.4 square meters and joins gates on either side.

Architect unknown, Summer Palace

Beijing
1894

Garden construction was a serious pursuit of Chinese emperors and private citizens since the last centuries BCE. Three Hills and Five Gardens became the popular name for scenic areas west of Beijing following renovation and construction under the Kangxi (r. 1661–1722) and Qianlong (r. 1735–1796) emperors. Qingyi (Pure Ripples), later renamed Yihe (Nurtured Harmony) Garden (yuan), the complex known in English as the Summer Palace, is the largest of the Five Gardens west of Beijing. It spanned 2.9 square kilometers.

Located on the former site of a Ming dynasty monastery, the Summer Palace was built by Qianlong between 1749 and 1764. He excavated Kunming Lake and added Wanshou (Longevity) Hill to the north to commemorate his mother's birthday. The lake occupied about three-fourths of the site. The Summer Palace was among the gardens demolished by British and French forces during the Second Opium War. In 1873, the Tongzhi emperor attempted to reconstruct it with the goal of a pleasure retreat where Cixi and Ci'an could retire. Funding was sufficient only for some repairs.

Cixi, however, used funds targeted to build the navy, with the pretense that naval exercises could take place on Lake Kunming. That Qianlong had built the gardens for his mother's sixtieth birthday and Cixi's sixtieth birthday had just occurred were other pretexts for the reconstruction. Cixi's marble boat in Lake Kunming became a symbol of her ill-advised excesses with Qing finances and a rallying point for anti-Qing protests in the late nineteenth and early twentieth centuries.

The residential complexes of Cixi and of Guangxu, Tongzhi's successor, comprised 3,000 structures and were completed in 1894. These included a three-story theater with seven trap doors on the stage, a 728-meter covered arcade, Seventeen-Arch Bridge, Jade Belt Bridge, Buddha's Incense Pavilion, and a bronze pavilion.

Architect unknown, Sheng Xuanhuai Residence

Shanghai
1896

Born in Wujin, Jiangsu province, Sheng Xuanhuai (1844–1916) came to work for Qing official Li Hongzhang in 1870. Through investments in shipping and other ventures, Sheng became the richest man in China. He held official positions under the Qing government in the Tianjin Customs Office, Ministry of Commerce, and Ministry of Post and Telecommunications. These appointments, in addition to his wealth, brought scrutiny of the Qing government as well as contact with foreign governments. Thus, when he became a strong advocate of modernization, Sheng feared government reprisals and fled to Japan. He returned to China after the fall of the Qing dynasty.

Although officially Sheng strongly supported keeping money in Chinese hands as opposed to giving it to foreigners, he paid an unknown Westerner for the design of his residence in Shanghai. The house is a three-story brick building with prominent pillars and a porch that spreads across the entire front.

1517

Heinrich Becker and Richard Steel, Russo-Chinese Bank

Tianjin
1896

The first Russo-Chinese Bank opened at the Russian embassy in Paris in 1895 for the purpose of lending money to China. The next year it opened branches in Shanghai and Tianjin. In 1902 it was the second-largest bank in China.

The two-story, yellow-brick building was located in the British Concession in the heart of Tianjin's financial district. It is distinguished by the use of yellow brick and its sharp contrast with the red dome above the corner entry. It is symmetrical from this corner, with pointed window frames on the first-story corner and arched frames above them here and reversed window framing along the sides. The dormers have a variety of frames, windows, roofing, and colors. The wooden support of the cupola is exposed, a common feature of Chinese domes.

赤峰桥
解放北路
禁止停车
电子监控摄录
关爱未成年人
呵护祖国花朵

V. V. Sakharov and others, City Hall

Dalian
1900

In 1898, Russia leased the Liaodong peninsula from the Qing dynasty and thereupon began construction of the city today called Dalian, Dal'ny in Russian. With an average annual temperature of 10 degrees Celsius, this most-distant port from Russia offered an opportunity for an ice-free commercial center.

Although Russian control lasted only seven years before falling to Japan as a result of the Russo-Japanese War (1904–1905), the Russian engineer, chief designer, and Dal'ny's first mayor Vladimir V. Sakharov (1860–1904), arrived in 1902 following his successful design of the port of Vladivostok. He became involved in the design of the city and many of its landmark buildings, ten of which survive along the 430-meter thoroughfare that is sometimes called Russian Street. City Hall was at one end of this street and Russian Library was at the other. The three-story structure with a pronounced central section and corners, covered by Mansard roofs that also cover two dormers on each side of the trapezoidal-shaped building, was a dramatic presence. However, before Sakharov could finish, the Russians were defeated by the Japanese. He subsequently set the building on fire. The Japanese repaired it and used it as a military headquarters. It later became a railroad office, hotel, hospital, and museum.

Architect unknown, Sheshan Observatory

Shanghai
1900

At the turn of the century, the French Catholic Mission built an observatory with two forty-centimeter refractive binocular telescopes with focal lengths of seven meters on the hill Sheshan, ninety-seven meters above sea level and twenty-five kilometers from Shanghai. French Jesuits had built the Xujiahui Observatory in Shanghai twenty-eight years earlier and rebuilt it in 1900. The Sheshan structure, now with the largest optical telescope in East Asia, overtook Xujiahui's capability. Weighing about three tons, the telescope was made in Paris in 1899 and installed here in 1901. It stands beneath a dome of ten meters in diameter.

Like all observatories, the one on Sheshan was built in part to accurately record time. It began transmitting time signals in 1954 and helped to establish China's first universal time-service network. The observatory successfully made atomic clocks in the mid-1970s. A forty-meter-high, brick-and-wood tower equipped with a Beckley-Robinson anemometer stands at the central top.

F. H. Schmidt,
Imperial German Post Office

Qingdao
1901

Germany issued its first postal stamps in Shanghai in 1886, in Tianjin in 1893, and in seventeen other treaty ports or concessions by 1904. Built between 1900 and 1901, the Imperial German Post Office in Qingdao issued its first postmark in 1905.
The three-story post office, with corner entrance, red tile roof, and green turrets included telephone and telegraph service, and an apothecary on the first floor. Upper stories were rented for other purposes. All German post offices in China closed in 1917 when China declared war on Germany. Today the building is a postal museum.

Architect unknown, Banque de l'Indo-Chine

Hankou
1902

Banque de l'Indo-Chine was founded in Paris on January 21, 1875, for the purpose of supporting French colonies in Asia. It opened offices in Saigon and Pondicherry in the same year. The first Chinese branch was opened in Shanghai in 1898, followed by offices on Shamian Island and Hankou in 1902, Tianjin and Beijing in 1907 and Kunming in 1910. The architecture of each of the branch buildings in China was as spectacular as the red-and-gray-brick Wuhan bank. The detailed white stonework above the central arches, four capitals atop the pillars on either side of the story-length arched windows, and the molding at the top of the facade of each front story contrast the green, vase-shaped balustrade railings above and below the second story and gray ribbon-like decorative band and twin bulbs atop posts on either side of it. Interestingly, the seven-bay structure with a widest central bay references the red-pillar-supported buildings that proliferated in China since the Tang (618–907) dynasty.

BANQUE DE L'INDO·CHINE

Pierre-Marie-Alphonse Favier, Dongtang

Beijing
1904

Dongtang (East Church), named for its quadrant in Beijing, is also known as Wangfujing Church (for its street address in this district of Beijing) and as St. Joseph's Church (for the patron saint of China). Its origins trace to German missionary Johann Adam Schall (1591–1666), who was given permission to build East Church and South Church by the Shunzhi emperor (r. 1644–1661). Four years after Shunzhi's death, East Church was destroyed. A church was rebuilt on the site in 1692, only to be destroyed in an earthquake that rocked Beijing in 1720. The third Dongtang, built between 1721 and 1728, was designed by Florentine Father Ferdinando Bonaventura Moggi (1684–1781). By the end of the Second Opium War, it had been severely damaged. Only a chapel replaced it. Plans to replace that structure with a grand church began in 1879 under Father Louis-Gabriel Delaplace (1820–1884). This fifth version was completed in 1884. The style is Romanesque Revival, marked by its symmetrical front facade, bold pilasters, and three domes. Chinese motifs include floral and vine patterns carved on the exterior. Destroyed during the Boxer Rebellion, it was rebuilt in the style of the fifth version in 1904. Pierre-Marie-Alphonse Favier, who designed churches in Tianjin and raised money for the reconstruction of Beijing's Church of the Savior (Beitang), designed this sixth version. During the 1950s the structure was used as an elementary school. It was renovated in 1980 and 2000.

天主堂
东堂

Wentrup, Police Station and Town Hall

Qingdao
1905

This building stands at the former intersection of Qingdao's European concession and its Chinese city. Like many German-built structures in Qingdao, this government headquarters, designed by a government architect, was marked by a high central tower. The six-story tower is centered not on the front facade but rather on the major thoroughfare, Munich Street, giving the structure a dramatic visual draw. The building has asymmetrical sides, one taller and narrower and the other low and wide.

It is further exceptional because the four-sided building stands on an octagonal site. Its steep, tile roofs and brick, grid-pattern gables are characteristic of the style known as German neo-Renaissance. The structure included residential space for Germans separate from the space for Chinese police. In 1908–1909, a rickshaw station with manufacturing and repair shops, as well as housing for drivers, was added to the site, a logical location since the train station was nearby.

W. Wutzler with G. L. Hempel, German Consulate

Hankou
1905

Enclosed by gardens whose plantings came from Japan as well as China, this German baroque structure with colonial-style verandas housed the consul and his family on the first and second levels. Service rooms were in the basement.

The kitchen and servants' quarters were in an adjoining building. The consulate's designer, W. Wutzler, belonged to the firm Selberg and Schlüter, which had offices in Berlin and Qingdao; Hempel was the site architect. The building's original four corner towers have been replaced, but its early-twentieth-century central tower with an eagle at its pinnacle remains.

Korbinian Paugger, Sacred Heart Cathedral

Jinan
1906

Built with Boxer indemnity funds, Sacred Heart Cathedral (Hongjialou) is an example of Gothic Revival architecture. It was designed by Korbinian Paugger (1855–1949), a Tyrolean Franciscan, in the manner of Notre Dame in Paris with a cross-shaped plan and two front steeples. Erected between 1901 and 1905, with additional construction in 1906, approximately 1,000 Chinese stone masons were involved in its construction, which was supervised by a mason from Jinan. The cathedral was closed in 1966 due to the Cultural Revolution, and its interior furnishings were dismantled. It was reopened on Christmas Day 1985.

Architect unknown, Qing Army and Naval Headquarters

Beijing
1906

In 1906, the Qing government built a new headquarters for its land forces and, shortly thereafter, a building in the same complex for its naval forces. The headquarters were behind a five-bay, pillar-supported entry with a ceramic-tile roof with overhanging eaves.

The army building, however, was brick, with a two-story front arcade punctuated by same-sized arched windows. At its center was a four-story clock tower flanked with three-story components. The naval headquarters also had a brick two-story central section and a two-story arcade of arched windows, as well as a flat front facade similar to that of an Italian baroque cathedral. The headquarters are an important example of imperial China's turn toward modern architecture in its last decade of existence.

Architect unknown, Guangdong Guild Hall

Tianjin
1907

Guild halls began to appear in Chinese cities in the Ming dynasty. Those who came to these halls in China, as in Europe, usually were merchants who brought their wares or put their skills to work in a province far from their homes. This guild hall served a population from Guangdong, more than 2,000 kilometers south of Tianjin.

The building's humble brick entry hardly prepares one for its interior, filled with intense and elaborate brick and wood carving and a spiraling dome. Built through the patronage of Tang Shaoyi (1862–1938), a Qing official and later diplomat and minister under Yuan Shikai and Sun Yat-sen, who was himself from Guangdong, the large, open, central banquet room has a stage on one side and sleeping areas on the other sides. The ceiling in the banquet hall was built to have optimal acoustic effects.

活水流花
嶺渤凝和
南金會萃

Architect unknown, St. Sophia Cathedral

Harbin
1907

Said to have been inspired by the Byzantine Christ the Savior Church in Birky, Ukraine, St. Sophia Cathedral is the largest Russian Orthodox Church in East Asia. It was built in wood in 1907, four years after the completion of the Trans-Siberian Railroad, which brought travelers and commerce from across North Asia to Harbin. The basilica was rebuilt in brick in 1911 and renovated and repaired between 1923 and 1932. Its tower has four bells of different sizes and tones. The four-story, 721-square-meter, cross-shaped building reaches 53.3 meters at the highest point, the pinnacle of the green, onion-shaped dome. It has entrances at both the front and back. Closed and then repurposed from 1958 to 1996, the church was restored in 1997.

家居建材旗舰基地

Mahike and Strasser, German Governor's House

Qingdao
1907

Sited at the top of a hill, the residence of the German governor was one of the most spectacular buildings in Qingdao. It was designed by Mahike under the direction of Strasser, Qingdao's director of public works between 1904 and 1907. Four features mark this building as belonging to the German Concession: the large, irregularly shaped-and-positioned pieces of granite; the sharp contrast between the granite and flat, painted areas; red and greenish roof tiles forming flat, painted, and curved sections; windows with posts running through them. These features as well as stone carving of knots, waves, chains, and a Viking dragon exemplify the Jugendstil (German art nouveau style). As at the German Consulate building in Hankou, the governor and his family lived on the first floor, guest quarters were on the second floor, and the kitchen was in the basement. After 1914, the house fell into Japanese hands, then was used by the mayor of Qingdao, and later was occupied by Mao Zedong.

Heinrich Becker and Carl Baedeker, German-Asian Bank

Jinan
1908

Deutsche Bank was founded in Berlin in 1870 for the purpose of fostering international trade. It opened its first Chinese branch in 1872 in Shanghai. In 1889 the name changed to German-Asian (Deutsche-Asiatische) Bank. New branches emerged in Shanghai, Kolkata, Tianjin, Hankou, Qingdao, Hong Kong, Yokohama, Kobe, Singapore, Beijing, Guangzhou, and Jinan. Although German interests in Jinan began after Germany colonized Qingdao in 1897, the Jinan branch of German-Asian Bank was built only after the completion of the rail line between Qingdao and Jinan in 1904.Shanghai-based Heinrich Becker (1868–1922) and Carl Baedeker were the architects for all German-Asian banks in China. Located next to the German consulate in the heart of Jinan's foreign commercial district, the building had red ceramic-tile roofs and a flat facade with scalloped tops, gables, and turrets, characteristics of the German neo-Renaissance style that was implemented in German concessions in the first decade of the twentieth century.

Architect unknown, Water Tower

Beijing
1908

Jingshi Tap Water Company was founded in Beijing in the aftermath of a fire in empress dowager Cixi's private quarters. The fire could not be extinguished because water could not reach the location fast enough. Cixi thereupon ordered construction of a water purification system run on steam engines that brought water into the full perimeter of Beijing.
Two sets of steam engines that could deliver 18,700 cubic meters of water a day were completed in 1910. Because of the fall of the Qing dynasty, the facility would not become operational until the Japanese occupation of Beijing. Today the water tower is part of the Tap Water Museum.

Atkinson & Dallas, Great Northern Telegraph Building

Shanghai
1908

In 1865, attempts to install a telegraph line between Beijing and Shanghai had been thwarted due to presumed negative effects on *fengshui* (Chinese geomancy). Five years later, a line was set up linking Shanghai, Hong Kong, China, and London. The Danish company Great Northern Telegraph, that in 1902 was one of the companies that laid telegraph wires across the Pacific Ocean, was a major contributor to placing telegraph wires in China. The Qing government official Sheng Xuanhuai, whose residence is discussed above, was instrumental in the telegraph's success. Great Northern Telegraph Building was designed by Brenan Atkinson and Arthur Dallas (1860–1924). In 1897, Atkinson had joined Dallas, Shanghai's chief municipal engineer, to form a firm that would build some of Shanghai's iconic buildings such as Banque de l'Indochine and Shanghai Land Investment Building. Dallas would serve in the Shanghai Municipal Council, was vice-chairman of the China Architects Society, and was a member of the British Royal Arts Society. The four-story, neo-Renaissance structure was built on the former site of a Russell & Company building. In 1922, Chinese Commercial Bank moved into the building. Since 1995, it has been shared by Bangkok Bank, the Royal Consulate of Thailand, and the residence of the Thai Consul General.

Architect unknown, Red Cross General Hospital

Shanghai
1909

In 1907, Shen Dunhe, a tea merchant and the founder of the Red Cross Society in China, established the Red Cross General Hospital, which opened in 1909. It was a teaching hospital of Harvard University from 1913 to 1918, thereby making it possible for Chinese doctors trained here to go to Harvard for further training. The hospital still maintains a relationship with Harvard Medical School. The building has a prominent central entry, corner towers, different windows across the first story and across the second, columns decorating the front facade, and shed roofs characteristic of Western architecture in China in the first decade of the twentieth century. The building became Huashan Hospital in 1956.

Scott & Carter, Palace Hotel

Shanghai
1909

Palace Hotel, designed by Walter Scott (1860–1917) of Scott & Carter, was the first hotel on the Shanghai Bund. Upon completion it was the tallest building in Shanghai, and it also had the first elevator in Shanghai. It stood on the site of Central Hotel, which had been constructed in 1875. The earlier hotel was not torn down until 1907, after the first phase of Palace Hotel was already standing. Famous events at the six-story, thirty-meter-tall, 120-room hotel include Sun Yat-sen's celebration of his presidency and the wedding of Chiang Kai-shek (1887–1975) and Soong Mei-ling (1898–2003).

OMEGA
OMEGA

Lothar Marcks & Busch, Bismarck Barracks

Qingdao
1909

Bismarck Barracks comprise four H-shaped buildings. Two of the barracks are made of granite; the others are brick; all of them have steep gables, red tile roofs, and flat front facades rising from solid, granite bases. These features, characteristic of contemporary construction in German concessions, lend solemnity yet elegance to the military barracks. The three-story dormitories had modernist features of steel frames, flush toilets, and basements. In 1945 the complex was used by US marines. Today the barracks are part of Haiyang (Ocean) University.

Architect unknown, Prayer Hall of Tianjin Great Mosque

Tianjin
1909

The design of Tianjin Great Mosque is typical of many mosques in China. The mosque was built in 1679 and expanded in 1801, and buildings were added to it in 1852, 1865, 1905, and 1909, when this prayer hall was constructed. The prayer hall and its front porch occupy 1,000 square meters and can hold about 1,000 worshippers.

The long, narrow structure is characteristic of mosques in China, as is its roof, which is of the *goulianda* (conjoined) style, consisting of a continuous covering above smaller sections. Much of the mosque was rebuilt in 1979, three years after an earthquake.

Architect unknown, Yokohama Specie Bank

Dalian
1909

Yokohama Specie Bank was founded in Yokohama in 1880. In 1884, the bank became the manager of Japan's foreign exchange and established an office in London before the end of the year. The first Chinese branch opened in Shanghai in 1893. Between then and 1945, there were thirty-four branches in China.

The bank closed in 1945. The symmetrical structure with a prominent center, three domes, the central one with eight ribs, and each with four circular windows, the varied window frames on the first story, second story, and corner towers, alternation of white strips against a beige background, and raised strips on the central section and on either side of the windows of the corner sections, clearly reference foreign construction in China, but more specifically, suggest France, England, and perhaps Russia.

Curt Rothkegel, Christian Church

Qingdao
1910

Born and educated in Germany, Curt Rothkegel (1876–1946) designed buildings for the German Concession in Qingdao as well as for the Chinese government in the first several decades of the twentieth century. Christian Church, also known as Christ's Church, was an opportunity to design a showcase monument: it stands on a hill that can be seen by ships entering the port. This location had been designated for a church when the Qingdao concession was planned.

Rothkegel won the commission through a competition. The tower he designed, a frequent feature in secular as well as church construction in China at the time, is thirty-six meters tall. Its belfry projects as it must, yet the building blends into the landscape because of the unfinished granite used on the variously shaped sections. The green top of the tower and the red ceramic roof tiles are typical of Jugendstil buildings in China.

Before working on Christian Church, Rothkegel designed Prince Heinrich Hotel Concert Hall in Qingdao in 1905. In 1910 he presented a design for the Imperial Consultative Assembly which would not come to fruition because of the fall of the Qing dynasty.

入口

Moorhead and Halse, Shanghai Club

Shanghai
1910

The Shanghai Club opened in 1864 with the purpose of being the most exclusive club in the city. President Ulysses S. Grant stayed there in 1877. By 1900, the club had nearly 1,000 members and more than 13,000 books in its library. In 1910, Moorhead and Halse rebuilt the club as a six-story, marble-faced, reinforced-concrete, Beaux-Arts building with two baroque-style cupolas and six ionic columns across the front center of the third and fourth stories and porches. The club's most noteworthy feature—the thirty-four-meter mahogany bar, the longest one known—was designed by Shimoda Kikutarō (1866–1931). Japanese members were permitted in the 1930s. Shanghai Club was taken over by the government in 1949, became a hotel again in 1971, and today is Waldorf Astoria Shanghai on the Bund. The bar remains.

Architect Robert Bradshaw Moorhead (b. 1865) came to China as a railroad engineer. In 1907 he formed a practice with Sidney Joseph Halse (1877–1946). Their most important buildings are the Shanghai Club and the McBain Building next door to it.

Architect unknown, Beijing Zoo Entrance

Beijing
1910

Since the time of the First Emperor, Qin Shi Huangdi (r. 221–210 BCE), Chinese emperors had game preserves. Public zoos, on the other hand, were European innovations. The history of Beijing Zoo dates to the last years of the Qing dynasty. In 1906, the Imperial Ministry established an experimental farm called Ten Thousand Animals Garden. The farm opened to the public in 1908. In 1911, the zoo became a national botanical garden. During the Second World War, many animals in the zoo died of starvation, and some of them were poisoned by the Japanese Army. The entrance is one of the parts that survives as it was in 1910.

票根专用
回收箱

Architect unknown, Bower of the Spirit Pool

Beijing
1911

The striking iron framework known as Lingzhaoxuan (Bower of the Spirit Pool) at the Palace of Prolonged Happiness (Yanxigong), today is an unfinished hall within the Palace Museum. It is evidence of a Qing-dynasty plan to build a modern version of a residence for concubines. Architecture in the Forbidden City had always been subject to fire, but the Palace of Prolonged Happiness had been plagued with conflagration. Fires occurred in 1802, 1832, 1845, and 1855. It was the most rebuilt palace in the Forbidden City. In 1909, the empress dowager Longyu (1868–1913) decided that this palace should be rebuilt as a Western-style building. Its materials were to be marble, brick, ceramic tile, and glass. All building materials, including the iron, were to be imported from England, Germany, and Belgium. The extraordinary three-story structure was to rise out of a pond, with the lowest level underwater so that residents could look out the glass windows to an aquarium. The water also symbolized protection from fire.

Aston Webb and E. Ingress Bell, Supreme Court Building

Hong Kong
1912

The first hearing of the Supreme Court in Hong Kong was in 1844, shortly after the city became a British colony. The building was designed by British architects Sir Aston Webb (1849–1930), once president of the Royal Institute of British Architects and president of the Royal Academy, who had designed the main building of the Victoria and Albert Museum, the front facade of Buckingham Palace, Victoria Law Courts in Birmingham, Britannia Royal Naval College in Dartmouth, and churches and palaces across the United Kingdom and E. Ingress Bell (1837–1914), who had worked with Webb in Birmingham, Dartmouth, and elsewhere. The two-story, granite, boldly symmetrical, neoclassical building with Ionic columns, and with a statue of the blindfolded Lady Justice at the top, is an example of a British structure intended to proclaim the presence of Great Britain in China. Except for the period of war with Japan, the most important cases in Hong Kong were heard here until 1997.

Later Jindai, 1912–1937

SOCIAL REFORM, ARCHITECTURAL MODERNIZATION

Chinese writers use the word *zhezhong zhuyi*, eclecticism, to describe architecture that was first seen in China in the 1900s and continued through the 1920s. A term also used to describe European and American architecture of the nineteenth and twentieth centuries, it refers to a building that incorporates identifying elements of more than one historical style, as well as ornamentation or motifs that may be from yet other styles. China was the recipient of these styles through architects from across Eurasia and America. Whereas most modern architecture in China through the 1910s was designed by British and occasionally French and North American architects, the postimperial years brought architects from all the nations who had fought China during the Boxer Rebellion: Austria-Hungary, Germany, Italy, Russia, Japan, France, England, and the United States. Construction increased dramatically after 1912 and especially after the First World War. The war as well as the revolution in Russia brought refugee architects to China.

The years from 1912 to 1928, when the Chinese government was in Beijing, are known as the Beiyang Period. Decades of unequal treaties and mistrust of Western ideas had forced a realization that China had to reckon with westernization, including the scientific inquiry that accompanied it. Architecture would be central to this realization, for until this time architecture that could be labeled "modern" had been designed by Europeans and Americans.

Some of the most dramatic changes on China's landscape occurred in Northeast Asia. Germany built intensely in Qingdao and elsewhere in Shandong and in Liaoning until 1919, when it relinquished its territorial rights to Japan. Russia built intensely in Harbin. Japan intensified an engagement with China that had begun in the late nineteenth century. Whereas Yamato (Japan) Hotels had been built in every major city where Japan had interests in past decades, Japanese colonial construction became grander and even more ambitious in the Northeast, the area that would be known as Manchukuo (Manchuria), where Japan gained additional territorial rights from Russia following the Russo-Japanese War of 1904–1905. Between 1912 and 1937, Japan focused attention on four cities, Shenyang and Dalian in Liaoning province, Changchun in

Jilin province, and Harbin in Heilongjiang province. Railway lines, industry, and new construction followed. Between 1932 and 1945, Changchun was called "new capital" (Xinjing). Before Japan left in 1945, architects constructed eight showcase government buildings with Sino-Japanese details that declared a new architectural modernism.

Even as much of North China fell to Japan in the 1930s, creative, sophisticated, and challenging design flourished in Shanghai and Nanjing. Chinese as well as foreign investors were patrons of urban architecture. The intense construction of universities, hospitals, and economic institutions that marked the 1920s turned more to apartments, hotels, theaters, and other places of private patronage. Nanjing was a major focus of new building because it was the capital of Chiang Kai-shek's Nationalist government from 1928 to 1949. Shanghai, where the Greater Shanghai Civic Center, the most ambitious design project of the decade, was implemented, became the backdrop for government activities. Before the end of the 1930s, however, most foreign architects practicing in Nanjing and Shanghai returned home. The Nanjing Decade, like the period division here, ended with Japanese attacks on China in 1937, whereupon the Nationalists retreated to Hankou.

Granite and concrete would dominate new architecture from about 1920 onward, especially in cities. In addition to unparalleled design and style, the potential of reinforced concrete for more durable buildings that required less replacement of damaged parts and were more easily fireproofed was realized. It would be followed in later decades by the use of steel.

THE 1910s

Upon defeat in the Boxer Rebellion, China owed reparations to eight foreign powers. The United States decided that rather than take the full amount, it would ask China to use a portion of the debt to fund education of Chinese students in areas critical to China's modernization. Architecture was among the crucial disciplines. Other nations would follow the lead of the United States, but none to as great an extent.

The Boxer Indemnity Scholarship Program was established in 1909. It funded the selection, preparatory training, transportation to the United States, and tuition at US universities for scholarship beneficiaries. This program included the establishment in 1911 of a preparatory school named Tsinghua College for Chinese students seeking to study in the United States. Classes were taught in English. The school later expanded to include four-year undergraduate and postgraduate programs, all antecedents to Tsinghua University today. China's First Generation of architects were awarded Boxer Scholarships at the Massachusetts Institute of Technology, Columbia, and Cornell, and the Universities of Illinois, Michigan, Texas, and Pennsylvania. The majority attended Penn and studied Beaux-Arts methodology with Paul Philippe Cret (1876–1945), who had been hired from L'École des Beaux-Arts in Paris in 1903 to train architects to design the grand, formal structures for which Beaux-Arts building was known. Liang Sicheng (1901–1972), often considered the most influential architect and architectural historian of the First Generation, studied with Cret and worked in his practice before returning to China.

THE 1920s

The decade of the 1920s began with the founding of the Chinese Communist Party and its first Congress in 1921. Sun Yat-sen's ascendancy in Guangzhou and continued support northward to Nanjing was halted by his untimely death in 1925, which gave way to sharper division of China into the Nationalists and Communists. The struggle would consume China for the next twenty-five years.

Foreign countries rescinded control of Chinese territories during this decade. In 1922, Japan returned Shandong to Chinese control. In 1924, China signed an agreement with the Soviet Union. England returned Hankou and Jinjiang to China in 1927 and Xiamen in 1930.

During this decade, China began to reap the fruits of overseas education from the Boxer Indemnity Scholarship Program. China's first Western-trained architects returned home with the mission and mandate to build a modern China and train students in modern design. The First Generation of architects also were China's first architectural historians, historic preservationists, and modern scholars of premodern architectural writings. Perhaps most impressive, this group of educated, urban elite made the first field trips to China's most remote regions and enlisted the help of locals to identify China's oldest standing architecture. Funding for their field surveys and scholarly publications came from the Society for Research in Chinese Architecture, which was established and largely funded by Zhu Qiqian (1871–1964), a Qing official turned Minister of Internal Affairs and Minister of Transportation under the Republican government. Zhu would become a member of the Committee of the Chinese People's Consultative Conference.

1927 was the beginning of the period of Chinese history known as the Nanjing Decade. It began when Chiang Kai-shek took Nanjing and made it the capital of the Nationalist (Guomindang [Kuomintang]) government. The next year, Nationalists centered in Hankou joined Chiang when the Beiyang government in Beijing fell.

THE 1930s

Civil war between the Communists and Nationalists began officially in 1931. It lasted eighteen years, until the founding of the People's Republic. In October 1934, Mao Zedong embarked on the year-long Long March west and then northward from Jiangxi to Yan'an in Shaanxi province. Also in 1934, Chiang Kai-shek gave his speech that promulgated life according to four Confucian principles, a doctrine known as the New Life Movement.

In October 1929, the Western world entered the Great Depression. However, China's economy, especially in Nanjing, continued to grow until 1931 when Japan invaded Manchuria and created the puppet state Manchukuo the following year. Japan would plan or re-plan city centers with visionary architecture that displayed every luxury and sometimes decadent amenities available in the 1930s for an East Asia-centered contemporary society. In China, industry flourished again from 1935 to 1936, part of the Nanjing Decade. In 1936, Chiang Kai-shek was taken prisoner by two of his generals. He was released two years later, giving way to a united front of Nationalists and Communists against the Japanese. The Marco Polo Bridge Incident on July 7, 1937, when China refused to let Japan beyond the bridge to search for a soldier, officially intensified the conflict.

By 1938, the Second Sino-Japanese War had led to forced relocations and closures in northern and eastern China. Universities and other research institutes where the First Generation worked along with the Society for Research in China Architecture left Beijing for Yunnan and then Sichuan. Architects and architectural historians from North and South China came together, joining in fieldwork and resulting publications about architecture in southwestern China. Many would not be able to return home until the end of the Second World War. In 1937, when China was on the verge of war with Japan, Chinese architects educated abroad as well as foreign architects designed across China.

Architect unknown, Lüshun Museum

Lüshun
1915

Lüshun, today a district of Dalian, passed from Japan to Russia and then back to Japan in 1905. It was named Port Arthur for a British Naval lieutenant who docked there in 1860, and Ryojun (Japanese for Lüshun) when controlled by Japan. By 1913, 9,000 Japanese lived there. Considered one of the most desirable ports in East Asia, China at one time considered using it to train its navy. Lüshun returned to the USSR after World War II, and then became China's in 1950.

The two-story Lüshun Museum boasts a Classical, central pediment, side windows with arched frames on the upper story and rectangular frames below it, and semi-circular corners. Excessive floriation alternates with two-level striated rectangular and trapezoidal patterns. The roof projects at four levels. Lüshun Museum was established in 1915 when the port was Japanese. The major exhibition was artifacts acquired in Central Asia on the expedition of Count Otani Kozui (1876–1948) in the first years of the 1900s.

旅順博物館

Architect unknown, St. Joseph's Cathedral

Tianjin
1916

Granted permission to build in 1912, begun in 1913, and completed in 1916, this largest church in North China became the French Catholic Mission. Located in the Tianjin neighborhood known as Xikai (Open to the Occident), the Romanesque-style cathedral, based on a Latin Cross plan, rises forty-two meters at its highest point, has an interior area of 1,892 square meters, and accommodates 15,000 worshippers. The domes are green copper, supported by wooden frames. Every brick used in the cathedral was sent from France. Red and yellow brick alternate on the exterior facade, and apertures are framed with white masonry. Windows are arched at the top and divided by columns. The cathedral was damaged in the earthquake of 1976 and subsequently repaired.

James R. Edmunds, Swasey Hall, Lingnan University

Guangzhou
1917

Lingnan University, today Sun Yat-sen University, began in 1888, when a Presbyterian missionary rented temporary quarters in Guangzhou. Martin Hall, a three-story, red brick building with verandas on the first and second stories, was built for the school in 1907. Swasey Hall, named for its patron from Cleveland, Ohio, was built in 1917. Designed by James R. Edmunds, Jr. (1890–1953) for the Shanghai-based Mission Architects Bureau, like other buildings on Lingnan campus, the architecture of Swasey Hall combines Chinese and Western features. The ceramic tile roof, lattice patterns on the porch railing, and bracket-set-shaped capitals of the central front columns reference China. The massive brick structure on a stone foundation conveys the permanence of Western design. Swasey Hall had an elementary school in its basement. Sun Yat-sen gave a speech in the hall in 1923; his death was mourned there fourteen months later.

Architect unknown, Mausoleum of Yuan Shikai

Anyang
1918

Yuan Shikai, the Qing general who became China's first president and, very briefly, emperor of China, was the son of a concubine. He thus was prevented from interment in his father's tomb. Yuan was buried at the place in Henan where he had lived from the death of Cixi until the fall of the Qing. The 90,000-square-meter, walled tomb is approached by a spirit path. It has ceremonial gates, a screen wall, and a stele pavilion modeled on the tomb of a Ming or Qing emperor. However, Western architecture is also present.

The mound is protected by reinforced concrete. Twelve stone lions that follow the style of European sculpture are carved on its perimeter. Iron gates supported on either side by stone pillars mark the front approach to the tomb.

Murphy & Dana,
Auditorium at Tsinghua College

Beijing
1921

In 1906, Henry Killam Murphy (1877–1954), in partnership with his Yale professor, Richard Henry Dana (1879–1933), opened a firm in Shanghai called Murphy & Dana. The firm was responsible for designing buildings on college campuses and churches across China, most of which were in the style known as adaptive architecture—that is, Western but adapting to China. However, the auditorium of Tsinghua College, where the majority of First Generation architects trained before studying in the United States, is purely Western. It resembles buildings in the style known as American Renaissance, such as Low Library at Columbia University, built by McKim, Mead & White in 1895–1897.

Atkinson & Dallas, Kailuan Mining Administration Building

Tianjin
1921

Only in Tianjin in 1921 would the headquarters of a mining company be a formidable example of Greek Revival architecture. Fourteen Ionic columns stretch across the front of the porch. Another fourteen Ionic columns, here marble with copper-plate capitals, dominate the center of the building's marble-walled, three-story, central room. A glass barrel-vaulted ceiling rises above it, and sections of its floor are mosaic. The structure was built for a company merged from Kaiping Mines and Luanzhou Mines, the first opened by Li Hongzhang for the Qing government in 1881 then taken over by the British, and the second opened in competition by Yuan Shikai in 1908. The merger took place in 1912. In the second half of the nineteenth century, the building was used by the Tianjin Municipal Party Committee.

Shattuck & Hussey, Peking Union Medical College

Beijing
1921

The Chicago-based firm Shattuck & Hussey, founded when Walter F. Shattuck (1871–1948) was joined by his student, Canadian Harry H. Hussey (1882–1967), began practicing in China in the 1910s. Peking Union Medical College is a brick and reinforced-concrete building unit capped by Chinese-style ceramic-tile roofs. This combination of Western and Chinese is an example of adaptive architecture. The medical school was funded by the Rockefeller Foundation in 1921 with the goal of being the best medical center in Asia.

Palmer & Turner, Hong Kong and Shanghai Banking Corporation Building

Shanghai
1923

HSBC Building was designed with two directives: no expense was to be spared and it was to dominate the Bund. It delivered both. At the time of construction, it was the most expensive building in Shanghai and the largest bank in East Asia. 50,000 tons of material were used. It took twenty-five months to complete. The neo-Classical structure is five stories tall with a seven-story central dome set on a triangular base. Six Ionic columns rise from the second to fourth stories across the front facade. The building has a steel frame, brick filling, and granite exterior. Inside, the dome displays the Greek gods Helios, Artemis, and Ceres. Below the dome are eight panels representing the cities most involved in Shanghai's international commerce during the period in which it was constructed: Shanghai, Tokyo, New York, London, Paris, Kolkata, Bangkok, and Hong Kong. Columns made from single blocks of marble tower in the main room. In 1923, the building had both heat and air conditioning. Special coins were minted for burial beneath the bank to enhance its auspiciousness.

The building's architect, George Leopold "Tug" Wilson (1880–1967), came to Shanghai in 1908 to work for the firm Palmer & Turner, founded in Hong Kong in 1868. Palmer & Turner was responsible for nine of the thirteen buildings designed for the Bund after 1920, six of which were designed by Wilson. During Japanese occupation, the bank became Yokohama Species Bank. In 1955 it became a local government building. Murals of the dome were slated for destruction at that time, but instead were covered, thanks to the recommendation of Penn-trained architect Benjamin Chen (Chen Zhi, 1902–2002). Today the building belongs to Shanghai Pudong Development Bank.

NEW YORK
SAPIENTIA
VERITAS

Rowland A. Curry, The Normandie

Shanghai
1924

The Normandie Apartments, also known as Wukang Mansion, is among at least forty structures designed by László Hudec (1893–1958) in Shanghai between 1925 and 1941. Born in Besztercebánya when it was part of Austria-Hungary, Hudec studied architecture in Budapest from 1911 to 1914. Captured and sent to a Russian prison camp in Siberia in 1916 during World War I, he escaped en route near the Chinese border. Hudec ended up in Shanghai, where he became one of the most important architects in the American firm of Rowland A. Curry (1884–1947). The Normandie was one of Hudec's last buildings in this practice. Hudec opened his own firm in Shanghai in 1925. At least thirty of Hudec's Shanghai buildings still stand. He left China in 1947, returned to Europe, and died during an earthquake in 1958, when he was teaching at University of California, Berkeley.

The Normandie is a corner structure with a triangular ground plan. The Flat Iron Building of 1902 in New York is said to have been its inspiration. Hudec's Normandie is six floors with three elevators and seventy-six apartments that ranged from efficiencies to multiroom suites. The first floor had a pedestrian arcade and shops. In 1929 there were fifty-one occupants and by 1939 there were 118. Today the building is preserved to appear as it did in the 1920s and is divided into ninety-five apartments.

Sun Zhixia, Nantong

Nantong
1926

In 1911, pro-modernization political reformer and entrepreneur Zhang Jian (1853–1926) hired architect Sun Zhixia (1882–1975), a native of Nantong, to take charge of the redesign of the city as a modern, Western-style metropolis on the Yangzi River. Sun designed several buildings as part of this plan, and his work continued until Zhang's death in 1926. Sun's premier design was Nantong Museum, considered China's first museum, although two buildings that housed natural history collections had been built in Shanghai in the late nineteenth century. In 1921, Sun designed Nantong Friendship Club, modeled after Club Concordia on the Shanghai Bund. He also designed Zhang Jian's residence, which had a European facade but Chinese interior details.

Charles Henry Gonda, Sun Sun Department Store

Shanghai
1926

Sun Sun was the third and largest of Shanghai's four great department stores, opening after Sincere (1914–1917) and Wing On (1918) and before Sun (1936). Sun Sun's owner S. K. Lau brought his experience doing business in Australia back to China. The store's architect, Charles Henry Gonda (1889–1969), was born in Hungary, educated in Vienna and Paris, and a prisoner of Russia in Ussuriysk during World War I, before coming to China. He designed more than twenty hotels, theaters, and banks in Shanghai from the early 1920s through 1941. Many of them stand today. Whereas Sincere and Wing On department stores had amusement parks on their top floors, Sun Sun had a sixth-floor radio station enclosed in glass around which shoppers could watch broadcasting six hours a day. The store also was known for a perfume ball from which fragrances dropped to anyone in a position to catch them.

海市第一食品商店
anghai First Foodhall
麦当劳
全季酒店

Shen Liyuan, Salt Industry Bank

Tianjin
1926

In 1909, Shen Liyuan (1890–1951) moved from Zhejiang to Naples to study math and physics. He went on to earn a degree in civil engineering at the Royal School of the Polytechnic University of Naples. Shen was the only First Generation architect to study in Italy. Like most First Generation architects, Shen had opportunities to design major buildings upon his return home. These included Salt Industry Banks, in Tianjin in 1926 and in Shanghai in 1928. The Tianjin bank is one of his few designs that survives. The asymmetrical structure has a prominent pair of pillars that suggest a corner entrance and yet, not positioned on a corner, a colonnade runs along only one side. In 1928 Shen began teaching at Beijing University, and from 1931 to 1934 he was chair of its Department of Engineering. He founded Tianjin Huaxin Engineering Firm. Shen wrote two books about geometric drawing.

中國工商銀行

Palmer & Turner, Customs House

Shanghai
1927

Along with the HSBC Building next to it, the Customs House is an iconic structure on the Shanghai Bund. Still a customs house today, it was the office of the British Governor-General in the 1920s. The light-red, brick-and-granite Greek Revival building has 32,680 square meters of floorspace spread over eight floors.

The clock tower that dominates the center of the structure is typical of customs houses in China. This one—with four faces, each 5.3 meters in diameter, using more than 100 pieces of glass, and said to be inspired by Big Ben in London—added three stories to the five-story base. The clock was designed by J. B. Joyce and Company in England, founded in 1690 and said to be the world's oldest clock maker. The clock tower is still the largest in Asia and houses the largest mechanical clock in Asia.

Palmer & Turner's Beaux-Arts building is the third customs house on this site. The first, built in 1857, had sloping Chinese roof eaves. The second was a red-brick Victorian building designed by Cory & Chambers in 1891. It was demolished in 1925 and replaced by this building, the tallest in Shanghai when it was completed.

The building's verticality, emphasized by the facade's four-story vertical walls topped by cubes of decreasing size, contrasts the horizontal sides and central dome of HSBC Bank that stands next to it. The pediments above arched windows on the corner towers, the art deco framing along the top of the main structure, base of the bell tower, and corner towers meanwhile respond to the pillar-supported pediment and smaller pillar-supported pediments and railings of HSBC Building. Inside, the first floor is lined with marble with gold leaf decoration and covered by an octagonal dome with mosaics depicting water commerce and the sea.

P
20分钟

Paul Müller, Quanyechang

Tianjin
1927

When it opened in 1928, the five-story Quanyechang was the largest department store in North China. It was named for a commercial showroom in Beijing that had been established in 1905 under the Qing dynasty. Beaux-Arts-trained Paul Müller of Hunke and Müller designed the building. Approximately 200 shops occupied 17,300 square meters of the 24,000-square-meter structure. Müller taught architecture and interior design at L'Institut des Hautes Études Industrielles et Commerciales de Tientsin (Tianjin).

Gao Xingqiao (1881–1948), later known as Xingqiao von Gao, of Nanjing, commissioned Quanyechang. He had begun his working life as a blacksmith, worked in a coal mine, became a sales manager, and by 1911 was the Chinese managing director of his company. In 1925, Gao decided to invest in commercial real estate. Quanyechang was his initial project. In 1931, sixth and seventh floors, known as the Eight Heavens, were added to the building. They had a bowling alley, theater, and teahouses. In 1992, Quanyechang again became a shopping center.

天津勸業場
迎駕洞藏 9
迎駕洞藏 20
STARBUC

László Hudec, Huadong Hospital

Shanghai
1926

The main building of Huadong Hospital, founded in 1921, was designed by László Hudec. He was commissioned by American businessman Charles E. Rayner who was living in Shanghai. His charge was for a hospital with all the amenities of those in the United States. There was no budget limit.

The 2,300-square-meter, five-story, neo-Classical structure, now known as the North Wing, is bilaterally symmetrical, with a double-column, open arcade on the ground floor and three shapes of windows—rectangular, circular, and arched—on the facade. The center front is unusual: the windows of the two lowest stories are closer to the front than those of the third and fourth stories, which are closer to the front than those of the highest story where a five-bay arcade is built. In September 2021, the hospital was elevated 1.2 meters to better preserve its foundation.

Palmer & Turner, Sassoon House

Shanghai
1929

The seventy-two-meter, 4,627-square-meter, art deco Sassoon House, formerly known as Cathay Hotel, later named Peace Hotel, and today the North Building of the Fairmont Peace Hotel, was commissioned by the Shanghai-based merchant and real estate developer Victor Sassoon (1881–1961) in 1926. It was planned as an office building but changed to a hotel while under construction. Its nine lower stories are the same width, and its upper three diminish in size. Its rooms along the Bund reflect Jacobean, Georgian, Indian, Chinese, Japanese, French, and 1920s interior design. A suite was named after British playwright Noël Coward (1899–1974), who spent a few days writing *Private Lives* there. The ballroom on the eighth floor was an international hot spot. The ninth and tenth floors had restaurants and private dining rooms.

Liu Jipiao, West Lake Exposition

Hangzhou
1929

French-educated Beaux-Arts student Liu Jipiao (1900–1992) was the main architect of West Lake Exposition, a world's fair where a fusion of art deco and Chinese architecture could be seen in Hangzhou for the first time. 20 million visitors saw 14,760,000 objects there over 137 days. Liu, with his colleague Li Fengmen, had already contributed designs at the Strasbourg Exhibition in 1924. Upon graduation in Paris in 1927, Liu returned to China and a year later co-founded the National Academy of Art in Hangzhou. He became a professor of art and architecture at Nanjing Central University in 1929. His firm designed in Shanghai, Nanjing, and Guangzhou, flourishing from 1932–1937. In 1937, Liu was put in charge of the fortification of Guangdong. He emigrated to the United States in 1947.

西湖博覽會博物館
全国重点文物保护单位
第一届西湖博览会
工业馆旧址
中华人民共和国国务院

Architect unknown, Arcade

Quanzhou
1930s

With a history of nearly a century, shopping arcades continued to be a feature of major cities across China in the 1930s. Quanzhou's is one of the best preserved. Shopping arcades are distinguished by pillars across the front so that the arcade is open to the street but covered to protect pedestrians from rain. Often stores are only at ground level and apartments are on every level above.

László Hudec, China Baptist Publication Building

Shanghai
1930

By projecting brown brick columns from a red-brick facade and recessing the bricks into a central tower, Hudec took the vertical thrusts of art deco architecture to new heights in this building. In addition to the publishing house, the China Baptist Publication Building accommodated warehouses, retail space, and offices, including Hudec's own office on the eighth floor. The structure exemplifies what was possible, perhaps uniquely, in Shanghai: a creative architect could design a work for a Christian publishing company that is worthy of international attention a century after its completion.

Architect unknown, Nankai High School

Tianjin
1931

Nankai High School was founded in 1904 by Yan Xiu (1860–1929), a Qing scholar-official who was engaged in national educational reform. The school moved to its current location in 1906. After the fall of Qing China, Yan did not take a position with the new government and instead focused his attention on the high school. Nankai was one of the first secondary schools in China to offer a Western, college-preparatory curriculum instead of the Confucian curriculum that had theretofore guided elite education, including Yan's. Like other elite secondary schools in China of the period, Nankai transitioned into a university. It regrouped to Chongqing following Japanese attacks. The school's most famous graduate was Chinese premier Zhou Enlai (1888–1976), who was a student from 1913 to 1917.

Nankai High School comprises four main buildings named for the cardinal directions plus important auxiliary structures such as an auditorium and dormitories. The two-story main buildings were constructed of wood and brick over three decades, from 1906 to 1931, and yet share defining features: four-sided windows on the first story, arched windows on the second story, arcades, and decorative orange exterior bricks. Fluted columns with Ionic capitals stand at the entrances of the earlier buildings, and raised, flat brick sections mark the facades of later buildings. Additional decoration includes Buddhist swastikas, swirling dragons, and plant motifs.

伯苓樓

Lü Yanzhi and Zhao Shen, Sun Yat-sen Mausoleum

Nanjing
1931

Sun Yat-sen died of cancer at Peking Union Medical College in January 1925. In April, an international competition for the design of Sun's tomb was announced. The charge was to make use of old Chinese forms, be special and commemorative, and create a new style based on the spirit of Chinese architecture. The 80,000-square-meter site was in Nanjing with Purple Mountain in the background, about two kilometers from the tombs of the founding emperor of the Ming dynasty and his successor. Even as Sun requested burial in this location so close to the Ming emperor's tomb, he also asked that his body be embalmed and exposed like that of Vladimir Lenin (1870–1924), as a symbol of the 1911 Revolution. A coffin was sent from Moscow, but it was not airtight, so this latter request was not fulfilled. Sun also requested that the tomb complex take the shape of a bell, a possible allusion to the Liberty Bell. The plan in fact takes that form. Visitors might see a comparison between the statue of Sun seated in his memorial hall with his writings engraved on the walls around him and Abraham Lincoln (1809–1865) in his memorial in Washington, D.C.

The winning design was by First Generation architect Lü Yanzhi (1894–1929), who graduated from Cornell with a degree in mechanical engineering in 1918 and had worked in the Murphy & Dana office. When Lü died during the construction of the mausoleum, First Generation architect Zhao Shen (1898–1978) saw the project to completion. Trees planted on the first anniversary of Sun's death correspond to statues that line the approach to the tomb of the Ming founder.

Lü Yanzhi, Sun Yat-Sen Memorial Hall

Guangzhou
1931

The 6,600-square-meter, octagonal memorial hall for Sun Yat-sen is dominated by a central auditorium, the largest in China until 1959. The focus of the steel and reinforced-concrete framework is the huge glass dome beneath the ceramic-tile octagonal roof and above the auditorium. No interior pillars block the view in the auditorium, which was designed to maximize its acoustics. The foundation and steps of the memorial hall are white granite, and the supporting pillars are red terrazzo, which exhibit a sharp contrast to the blue-glazed tile roof.

Guan Songsheng, Zhu Bin, and Yang Tingbao, Central Stadium

Nanjing
1931

Central Stadium originally joined seven other stadiums on its site, making it the largest sports complex in East Asia at the time. The colonnade of archways that enclose Franklin Field at the University of Pennsylvania, where architect Yang Tingbao (1901–1982) studied, may have inspired the design of Central Stadium, although Guan (Kwan) and Zhu Bin (Chu Pin) had not seen the Penn campus. Both stadiums are made of brick and both have smaller arched windows above those of the lower level. The Nanjing structure transposes an American stadium inspired by Beaux-Arts and art deco design into a modern Chinese structure that seats 60,000. A triple-arched entrance can be viewed as equivalent to the wide, central bay of a Chinese building, with symmetrical side bays, that are standard in Chinese timber construction; six brick pillars extend from the ground to above the top of the facade behind them, like wooden pillars; a balustrade along the upper level mimics lattice patterns of South China; corner towers have Chinese-inspired lattice patterns at the tops; and Chinese-roofed pavilions punctuate the top.

Architect unknown, Trinity Catholic Church

Dali
1931

Christianity probably arrived in Yunnan province during the period of Mongolian rule, but it had a continuous presence only beginning in the Qing dynasty. French missionaries were in Yunnan by 1753. Father Pierre Erdozaincy-Etchart (1883–1931), head of the Dali Diocese, oversaw construction of Trinity Catholic Church from 1927 until his death. The church is timber framed with brick and plaster walls, and it has a belfry at its center. Its 600-square-meter single room could hold 500 worshippers.

The four-arm bracket sets and more than ten sets between pillars are features of Qing timber framing. The broadly sloping roof eave corners are characteristic of traditional architecture in South China, and the fluted stone pilasters also have a long history in premodern China. Details of the structure, particularly elephants and lions, reference southwestern China. They also include stories from the Bible and legendary Chinese heroes. The church is evidence that as late as 1931 the Chinese timber frame that defined architecture as Chinese could be used for a church as well as for a Buddhist or Daoist temple.

Architect unknown, Chefoo Club

Yantai
1931

This club for Westerners was first built in 1865, when there were fifteen consulates in Yantai. It was expanded in 1907 and enlarged again in 1931. The additive structure with dormers across the top story, one flat facade, a circular room, and a Chinese pavilion had the standard amenities of a European men's club as well as a ballroom and racetrack.

Poy Gum Lee, Robert Fan, and Zhao Shen, Young Men's Christian Association Building

Shanghai
1931

Born in Chinatown, New York, and educated at Pratt Institute, MIT, and Columbia, Poy Gum Lee (Li Jinpei; 1900–1968) worked for Henry Murphy before moving to China in 1923. A Young Men's Christian Association building had been built in Shanghai in 1900. This 1931 YMCA building was one of Lee's major commissions in China. Before he returned to the United States in 1945, Lee worked on eleven YMCA and YWCA buildings in China. When Lee had an opportunity to participate in the building of Sun Yat-sen's Mausoleum, following the death of Lü Yanzhi, the Shanghai YMCA was completed by Robert Fan and Zhao Shen, both of Allied Architects, a firm they had founded with Penn Architecture classmate Tong Jun (1900–1983) in Shanghai in 1930. When completed, the YMCA building had nine stories.

All three architects associated with the Shanghai YMCA sought to successfully blend Chinese architecture and international modernism. The under-eaves bracket sets, imitation lattice windows, eight-pronged patterns on the upper architraves, roof rafters, tile, and floral patterns carved into the frame of the archway above the central entry reference China. The second floor's coffered ceiling and the verticality and uniformity of window shapes reference modernism. The building had offices, lecture rooms, game rooms, an exhibition hall, two banks, a swimming pool, a club lounge, a café, and 250 rentable rooms. Robert Fan was disappointed with the results. After completion of the YMCA, he turned to more exclusively art deco or other modernist designs. Today most of the YMCA building is used as a Jinjiang Hotel.

METROPOLO
JINJIANG HOTELS CLASSIC
锦江都城经典青年会酒店
青年會

Palmer & Turner, Grosvenor House

Shanghai
1932

This magnificent art deco building towers eighteen stories, the vertical thrust of its central walls starkly contrasting the stories of apartments that spread horizontally on either side. Inspired by skyscrapers in Manhattan, Grosvenor House was the first skyscraper to stand in Shanghai, and it was built on swampland. Shanghai entrepreneur Viktor Sassoon funded the project. He intended to achieve a structure more luxurious than his Sassoon House. Clawfoot bathtubs and parquet floors were among the amenities.

Bright Fraser (b. 1894), educated in England and an architect in Shanghai Land Investment Company, echoed much of Grosvenor House in his work on Broadway Mansions, which was designed by Palmer & Turner between 1932 and 1934. Fraser said the structure took inspiration from the Chinese character *ba*, meaning eight, whose two strokes curve diagonally from the top center.

Charles Henry Gonda, Cathay Theater

Shanghai
1932

This 1,080-seat, single-level, art deco theater opened in 1932 with the film *A Free Soul* starring Norma Shearer (1902–1983). At one time the theater was owned by Viktor Sassoon. The facade treatment at the corner, which is dominated by vertical panels of glass posed between brick and cement, extends to its adjacent street facades. The central panel soars starkly toward the top where it announces a circular, brick, windowed section. The theater is in operation today.

Yang Tingbao, Musical Stage

Nanjing
1933

This musical stage is a profound example of Yang Tingbao's ability to blend Chinese and non-Chinese architecture into a unique structure. Stages for musical performance had been built in China since the first millennium BCE, but until Yang's design, no one in China had constructed an amphitheater. Yang thus drew from ancient Greece and Rome in this design, then implemented a screen with a Chinese wave pattern and dragons emerging from the waves, a lotus pond with goldfish, and a fountain. The 4,200-square-meter, open-air stage is across from the approach to the Sun Yat-sen Mausoleum.

Charles Henry Stableford and Arthur Carr Wheeler, Shanghai Municipal Council Abattoir

Shanghai
1933

Stableford (1863–1944) and Wheeler's building was the largest slaughterhouse in Shanghai and one of the three largest in the world at the time it was built. Its front facade features a taller central section, a ubiquitous feature in 1920s and 1930s Shanghai. The front arcade, curved ceiling, and latticework panels hardly suggest an animal processing plant. The turns and bends of the thickly poured industrial concrete, the maze-like interior and stairs on each level, and the fifty-centimeter-thick walls, however, that confuse and slow down the path of animals who might want to escape are not visible from the outside. 300 mostly umbellate beams and twenty-six bridges branch and span spaces from the first upward. The windows in the west are interpreted as leading to the Western paradise of the Buddha, where all sentient beings could be received.

Some 1,200 animals were slaughtered here every day. Creatures entered on the first floor and were driven up ramps, and then penned on upper levels. Pigs were kept on the ground floor because they would not run up the ramps quickly. Animals were slaughtered upstairs, then lowered for butchering. There was an area for cold storage. Waste, diseased meat, and unusable body parts were carried to an incinerator across the street. Today the complex is known as Old Millfun. It is a shopping mall with restaurants and entertainment venues, and the water tower at the top has been transformed into a ballroom with a glass floor.

Spence Robinson & Partners, Race Club

Shanghai
1933

Shanghai had a racetrack and race club in 1848, almost as early as it became a concession. The track of 1862, on the location that would house the track in 1933, was the third one in the city. It may be the only racing venue marked by a ten-story bell tower, a structure identifying the building more as a monument of an international city in China than as a clubhouse. Inside, the clubhouse had marble staircases, teak paneled rooms, and oak parquet floors. Bets were taken on the first floor, one could bowl on the mezzanine level, and club members watched the races, dined, and had rooms on the second floor. Japan occupied the Race Clubhouse in 1941, and racing continued at the site until 1945. Today the building is the Shanghai History Museum and the race course is People's Park.

Liu Shiying, Wang Boqun Residence

Shanghai
1934

This spectacular, three-story, forty-room, 2,330-square-meter, Victorian Gothic structure was built for forty-six-year-old Wang Boqun (1888–1944), Minister of Communications for the Guomindang and president of Daxia (Great China) University, and his twenty-two-year-old bride. From 1941 to 1944, a Japanese official lived in the house, and then it was a Guomindang prison, then offices of the British Consulate, and from 1949 on a Children's Palace. The building's architect, Liu Shiying (1893–1973), had studied at Tokyo Higher Technical School and returned to China to found the Architecture Department at Suzhou University with Liu Dunzhen (1897–1968), who also had studied in Japan. Liu Dunzhen went on to join Yang Tingbao and Tong Jun as the leaders and shapers of the study of premodern Chinese architecture at Nanjing University, and then at Southeast University in Nanjing.

László Hudec, Park Hotel

Shanghai
1934

The twenty-two-story Park Hotel, with two additional stories underground, was intended to be the tallest building in East Asia. It maintained that status in China until 1966 and in Shanghai until 1983. Because it stood on swampland, László Hudec used reinforced pilings to support the building's great weight. Hudec is said to have taken inspiration from the twenty-three-story American Standard Building on West 40th Street in Manhattan as well as the art deco buildings that were popular in China at the time. The first three floors of Park Hotel use polished black granite from Shandong. The floors above use brown brick faced with ceramic tile. The penthouse nightclub had a retractable roof. The hotel was renovated in the 1980s, in 1997, and in 2001.

Hudec's Grand Theater down the road was the largest and most elegant of Shanghai cinemas. With the Park Hotel, it brought international architectural recognition to Shanghai. Both were featured in leading Western architectural periodicals such as *Baumeister* and *L'Architecture d'Aujourd'hui*. Hudec's work includes schools, churches, offices, residential blocks (including the first multi-tenant block of luxury apartments in China), industrial complexes, including the Shanghai Waterworks, and Union Brewery, the biggest brewery in China at the time.

Yang Ximiao, Paramount Ballroom

Shanghai
1934

Businessman Gu Liangcheng hired architect Yang Ximiao (S. J. Young, 1899–1978) to design the most fashionable nightclub and dance hall possible. Yang chose the popular art deco style, with its prominent, curved entry and projecting tower above it. Paramount Ballroom was completely air conditioned. This largest ballroom in Shanghai had two dance floors, one glass and lit from below and the other made of shock-absorbent wood, as well as rotating mirror balls and flashing colored lights. Neon strips on the exterior flutes lit up at night. Charlie Chaplin visited in 1936, the same year Gu went bankrupt. Stories that the ballroom was a den of iniquity proliferated; it closed in 1956.
It reopened as Red Capital Cinema and closed again during the Cultural Revolution. It was renovated several times for use as a ballroom or nightclub in the twenty-first century.

PARAMOUNT

Palmer & Turner, Metropole Hotel

Shanghai
1934

The fourteen-story Metropole Hotel was designed by the same firm (Palmer & Turner) and had the same patron (Viktor Sassoon) as those for the Hamilton House across the street. The art deco curves of the fronts of both buildings mirror each other. Sin Jin Kee Contractors were the Metropole's builders, and it was completed in only three months—very quick for a high-rise building in Shanghai. Metropole Hotel was one of the earliest Shanghai buildings to use Airconcrete, a method patented in Germany in 1889 of aerating concrete with carbon dioxide; it resulted in a much lighter material than poured concrete but was equally solid.

METROPOLO

Veysseyre & Kruze, Gascogne Apartments

Shanghai
1934

The Gascogne Apartments are separated into two: a five-story building fronting the street and a thirteen-story building behind it, rising to fifty-three meters. The vertical, central walls and curved sides identify the building as 1930s art deco. Windows on the circular corners as well as on the walls and arcades allow for maximum light in the steel-framed structure.

Gascogne Apartments was designed by Beaux-Arts trained Paul Veysseyre (1896–1963) and Alexandre Léonard (1890–1946). In 1922 they opened a practice on the Bund. Leonard Kruze joined them in 1933; the firm became Veysseyre & Kruze. Like the offices of László Hudec, those of Veysseyre & Kruze were in one of their own buildings. The firm's most significant buildings were art deco style and designed in the mid-1930s. Veysseyre left China in 1937 for Saigon, where he opened a branch office.

LAWSON
便利店
GAIA
HAIR

Zhuang Jun, Shanghai Mint

Shanghai
1935

The first Chinese mint was established in Shanghai in 1920. Intended to be the largest mint in the world, it remained in Shanghai even after the mint became part of Beijing's National Ministry of Finance. Retaining the Shanghai location was perhaps symbolic of the city's importance in international business. The boldly symmetrical Beaux-Arts Shanghai Mint has six columns supporting a pedimented entry bracketed by two towers, shorter corner towers, three stories across the center, two stories on the sides, and shorter windows on the top story than the lower ones. Zhuang Jun (1888–1990) designed the building, and Philadelphian Clifford Hewitt (1869–1942), an engineer and adviser on mint design who had worked on the mint in Manila before coming to Shanghai, supervised its construction. Hewitt spent ten years in Asia.

上海造幣

Yang Tingbao, Dahua Movie Theater

Nanjing
1935

This 1,070-seat cinema is considered Chinese art deco. Its designer, Yang Tingbao, was not as concerned about stylistic identity or allegiance as some architects of his generation. He was aware of the many theories and schools of design around him, yet he was known for responding to the space available and what could be achieved there. The theater's modest exterior and simple rectangular floor plan confirms this. Inside, the huge lobby features a grand staircase and a pair of massive, boldly decorated columns, whose fluted capitals with entwined vines are reminiscent of West Asian architecture. The interlocking L-shaped pattern just below them has a history in China since the early Common Era. A semicircular panel inset into a low wall in front of the pillars is decorated with Chinese latticework.

Dong Dayou, China Aviation Association Building

Shanghai
1935

This concrete building is best known for its airplane shape, but it is in fact a significant art deco structure designed by First Generation architect, Dong Dayou (1899–1973), who was educated at University of Minnesota and Cornell and practiced in Chicago before returning to China in 1928. Dong was responsible for much of the design of the Greater Shanghai Civic Center, of which this was a part. The spectacular building is entered at the nose of the plane, a three-story, circular atrium topped by a circular dome with colored glass inlays. Stairs wrap around the atrium to access the museum and library. The body and tail of the plane house offices. The building was renovated in 1993.

Endo Arata, Central Bank

Changchun
1935

Educated at Tokyo Imperial University, Endo Arata (1889–1951) later studied with Frank Lloyd Wright (1867–1959) at Taliesin, and then worked in Wright's studio in Tokyo. In Japan, Endo's Koshien Hotel exemplifies his Wright-inspired work. As an architect in China during the Manchukuo period, Endo designed Central Bank. Its front facade—with ten fluted columns flanked by stark, vertical rectangles—perhaps references Wright's affinity for horizontality, and the stylized-M-shaped decoration along the top of the portico perhaps references art deco. But at the same time the structure reflects Beaux-Arts-transformed modernism of the Changchun era. Unlike official buildings of the Manchukuo government, Central Bank does not reference premodern Japanese construction.

Aiga Kensuke and Ishii Tatsuro, Ministry of Justice and State Council Building

Changchun
1935 and 1936

The Ministry of Justice is one of the Eight Great Ministries (Badabu) in Changchun, the capital of the Japanese-occupied state in northeastern China known as Manchukuo. The three upper stories of the four-story central entry reference Japanese architecture of the sixteenth- or seventeenth-century castle through the use of ceramic-tile roofing on gable-ends, but here the feature is at the front rather than the side of the roof. A middle row of three windows with ogee arches perhaps references the Japanese gable type known as *karahafu*. The clock embedded in a sash-like hanging may be inspired by *gegyō*, the "hanging fish" that is suspended from a Japanese gable. This feature of a side gable, shown from the front above a portico, would be employed at Tokyo National Museum in 1937, at Yuzhno-Sakhalinsk Museum in Sakhalin, Russia, in 1937, and at Gaoxiong Station in Tainan in 1941.

Others of the Eight Great Ministry buildings became parts of schools. The red-brick Ministry of Transportation building, now part of the Jilin University College of Public Health, rises above the rest as the center of all the Eight Great Ministries. The State Council Building, designed by Ishii Tatsuro, became part of Bethune Medical College, named after Canadian Henry Norman Bethune (1890–1939), a thoracic surgeon and Communist who came to Yan'an during the Second Sino-Japanese War. After Bethune died of sepsis following treatment of a patient on the battlefield, Mao Zedong gave the eulogy at his funeral. His statue stands in front of the college.

诺尔曼·白求恩大夫
Dr. Norman Bethune
1890 —— 1939

Luke Him Sau and Palmer & Turner, Bank of China

Shanghai
1936

In 1928, Bank of China moved its headquarters from Beijing to Shanghai. The new building on the Bund was to be symbolic of the bank's desire to have a strong presence in the highly competitive commercial city. From the beginning, the building was constricted by finances and physical space. More a people's bank than many operating in China in the 1920s, Bank of China had less foreign investment than the banks with which it competed. The bank set aside money for six years to pay for the building, finally beginning construction in 1934. However, its plans for a thirty-four-story structure had to be amended.

Viktor Sassoon's Sassoon House (Cathay Hotel) was next-door, and Sassoon refused to allow any building to rise higher than it. The British City Council in Shanghai approved Sassoon's wish; the roof of Bank of China is about one foot lower than the highest point of the hotel. The imitation bracket sets and a ceramic-tile roof with dramatically sloping corner eaves were the designers' response to the bank's desire for some aspect of the architecture to identify it as Chinese. Stylized characters *shou* (longevity) are carved into the brickwork on either side of the tall, vertical, central facade. Like most buildings on the Bund, the Bank of China had apartments on its upper stories. Luke Him Sau (Lu Qianshou, 1904–1991), born in Hong Kong and educated in Britain, and local firm Palmer & Turner contributed to the design. Because of the War with Japan, Bank of China did not move into this building until 1946.

中国银行 BANK OF CHINA

Hunke & Müller, Bohai Building

Tianjin
1936

This modernist building—exemplified by its vertical thrust, sleek panels of windows, and central tower—was the tallest building in Tianjin at its time. Commissioned, like Quanyechang, by Gao Xingqiao and designed by Paul Müller of Hunke & Mülller, it rose 47.5 meters at its highest point. Named for Gao's son, Gao Bohai, who managed the structure, Bohai Building has eight stories plus two additional stories in the tower. It is made of the highly fireproof material reinforced concrete and covered with a tile facing. Stairs zigzag through a stairwell from the first through eighth story. The five-sided building, with only one corner presenting as a 90-degree angle, is divided into shops, offices, and residences. Bohai Building often is compared to Leopold Building, a five-story, corner-facing brick commercial and residential structure designed between 1936 and 1938 by Müller for the Swiss investor Marcel Leopold (1902–1957).

Allied Architects, Moller Villa

Shanghai
1936

British-Swedish merchant Eric Moller (d. 1956) came to Shanghai in 1919 to expand a shipping business begun by his father in Hong Kong, China in the 1860s. He eventually made a substantial fortune in shipping, real estate, and horse racing. In 1936, he commissioned Allied Architects for the design of this villa. The Northern European style used here was said to have been inspired by a sketch Moller's daughter made of a castle she had read about in a fairy tale. Details incorporate nautical themes to reference the family business. The villa took ten years to complete. After the Mollers left Shanghai, the building became the headquarters of the Communist Youth League. In 2002, it became Moller Villa Hotel, with eleven guest rooms in the old house and thirty-four in a new section.

F. H. Kales, Wuhan University Campus

Wuhan
1936

MIT-educated F. H. Kales (1899–1979) designed college campuses in China in the late 1920s and 1930s. In October 1929, he was hired to design his largest architectural project to that time, the 213.3-square-hectometer campus of Wuhan University, one of China's first national universities, which had been founded in 1893. Kales designed twenty-six buildings that are still in use. The work was divided into thirty projects, thirteen of them finished between 1920 and 1923, and another seventeen between 1932 and 1937, after which there was not enough money to continue. Kales sought a mixed Sino-Western style on the campus. Chinese critics said the architecture was satisfactory, but the colors were not Chinese. The Japanese used the buildings as military headquarters in 1938.

Graham & Painter, Liza Hardoon Building

Shanghai
1938

This structure was designed by British architect Percy Tilley (1870–1947) of Graham & Painter and was described as the most up-to-date structure in Shanghai at the time. Like other art deco buildings in the city, its center front was prominent but not flat, made primarily of reinforced concrete, and it had a stone exterior and steel doors and window frames.

The entire structure was built in less than a year. The building was named for the richest woman in Asia at the time, Liza Hardoon (Luo Jialing, 1864–1941), wife of investment tycoon Silas Hardoon (1851–1931). It housed some of the most important offices in Shanghai, including those of Chase Bank.

ICBC 中国工商银行

Makino Masami, Supreme Court

Changchun
1938

One of the last of the Eight Great Ministries of Manchukuo's capital to be completed, the Supreme Court was built with a central section that was several stories taller than the rest of the structure. In this way it is like so many modern buildings in Changchun and across China constructed in the 1930s. Yet its design is unique. The tall section has four tri-lobed corners, the central of the three lobes larger than the other two, and curved corners at every point where a wall joins a wall. Each level of the structure had a Chinese-style ceramic-tile roof, except for the division between the third and fourth stories across the front, which can be described as art deco. Like other 1930s structures in China, the Supreme Court uses varied materials on different stories, but its rows of windows are less varied. Today the building is a hospital.

人民大街
下一出口

László Hudec, D. V. Woo Residence

Shanghai
1938

This four-story residence was nicknamed Green House for two reasons: its exterior is made of green-glazed tile, and its owner, dye magnate D. V. Woo (Wu Tongwen) said that green, the color of Nationalist uniforms, was his lucky color. Woo had received the land where the house stands in 1927 as dowry for his very wealthy Suzhou bride. By 1935, the year he commissioned László Hudec to design the building, his wife and concubine had added many children to his household. Hudec sought to implement the most up-to-date Western technology and style in the Woo Residence. It was the first private residence in China that had an elevator, gas heat and cooling, including hot water in the bathrooms, spring floors under the dance hall, and a driveway leading to a ground-level garage. It had a billiard room, bar, and European-style dining room; and yet in deference to Chinese tradition, it had an ancestral hall. The nearly circular corner is made with curved glass to draw maximum light into it: it functions as a four-story sunroom. Balconies were of decreasing width from the ground level to the top floor. This would be one of Hudec's last commissions in Shanghai.

LINE 2/7

Late Jindai, 1937–1949

MODERN CONSTRUCTION DURING POLITICAL UPHEAVAL

There are few periods of twelve years in which as much has happened in one country as 1937–1949 in China. No one in China was spared the turmoil. It was China's fourth decade of civil war, but for part of this period, the internal fighting was less intense than it had been in earlier times because of a united effort against Japan. In the global arena, the decade is considered split between before and after 1945, the year the Second Sino-Japanese War ended.

Carnage during this period was intense. The Nanjing Massacre by Japanese troops that resulted in some 200,000 deaths from December 1937 through January 1938 was followed fewer than two years later by the Hundred Regiments Campaign of the Communists in North China, against which the Japanese retaliated in the Three-All (kill, burn, loot) Campaign that included biological warfare and resulted in tens of thousands of deaths. Starvation was equally a killer. In 1942 and 1943 there was intense famine, especially in Henan province.

Globally, the end of World War II was preceded by the Yalta Conference in February of 1945 where Franklin Roosevelt, Winston Churchill, and Joseph Stalin anticipated victory in Europe and determined that the Soviet Union's engagement in war in the Pacific would bring Sakhalin Island (located between Khabarovsk province of Russia and Japan's northern island Hokkaido) as well as a continued lease of Port Arthur and interest in rail lines in Northeast Asia to the USSR. A result of the end of the War with Japan in 1945 was the return of Taiwan to China. 1945–1949 was the most bitter period of China's internal warfare. It ended when Mao Zedong became chairman of the People's Republic of China and Chiang Kai-shek and several million followers set up a Nationalist government in Taiwan.

THE 1940s

Construction in China was limited between 1937 and 1945. When war with Japan ended, architectural projects begun before the war could be completed. Building flourished during these years in Manchukuo where Japan continued to construct magnificent civic architecture that represented their vision of a contemporary East Asian city, particularly in Changchun. The years 1945–1949 were a period of both construction and creativity in China. Commemorative architecture became a new focus of postwar building. Architects turned to European masters Le Corbusier (1887–1965) and Bruno Taut (1880–1938) and incorporated their ideas into Chinese buildings. Modernism, which had been focused primarily in Shanghai and Nanjing in the 1930s, became a stylistic option throughout the country. References to Chinese traditions, such as big roofs, continued to be used in civic construction.

Architect unknown, Jinmu Hall

Changchun
1940

The year 1940 was three years after the Marco Polo Bridge Incident that marked the official beginning of the Second Sino-Japanese War. It was also the 2,600th anniversary of the official founding of Japan by Emperor Jimmu (r. 660–585 BCE). This white-washed headquarters of the Japanese government and residence of the ambassador commemorated him. The gray ceramic-tile roofs and eaves, positioned at the front as well as the standard gable sides, referenced Japanese castle architecture.

Robert Fan, Majestic Theater

Shanghai
1941

The 1,597-seat theater held more than 200 live performances, concerts, and movies every year. It had extraordinary acoustics. Its Chinese name, Meiqi (beautiful jade), was chosen through a public competition; it was called Majestic in English because the names sounded similar. Five long, narrow windows define the entrance as art deco style as well as mark the spiral staircase that runs through the full-height entry hall behind it. The facade recalls that of Paramount Ballroom, built in Shanghai seven years earlier. The Majestic was one of the first theaters in China to show Western movies. After 1945, the building held more live performances than films. Majestic Theater was restored in the 2010s.

MAJESTIC
美琪大戲院
AJESTIC THEATRE

Shang Qixu, Nanyue Martyrs' Shrine

Hengyang
1943

Hengyang in Hunan province is the location of the sacred Southern Marchmount (Nanyue). In 1937 a battle with the Japanese occurred there, and in 1938 Nationalist leader Chiang Kai-shek and Communist leaders met there to confirm the united front necessary to defeat Japan. The shrine was completed on July 7, 1943, six years after the battle whose dead soldiers it commemorates.
The shrine is laid out like a Tibetan-Buddhist-Chinese monastery, such as Temple of the Azure Clouds (Biyunsi) in the Fragrant Hills of Beijing: the approach and front of the complex comprise courtyards (240-by-70-meters) on flat ground; the back areas are forested.
Its trees are pines, Chinese symbols of longevity. The shrine is marked by five bombshells pointing upward and symbolizing the unity of China with the Han people at the center and Manchu, Mongol, Hui (Chinese Muslims), and Tibetan people represented around them.
Thirteen mausoleums contain the remains of Chinese soldiers who died here. Paying homage to them is also an opportunity to pay homage to the sacred peak.

Zhuan Xueren, Ma Bufang Mansion and Ma Buqing Mansion

Xining and Linxia
1943 and 1945

The 6,000-square-meter mansion was built for Nationalist General Ma Bufang and his family from 1942 to 1943. Ma was a Chinese Muslim who came from Linxia, a region of Western China adjacent to Xining. The architecture is typical of a traditional, Chinese residence of multiple courtyards befitting a high-ranking member of the Guomindang. Ma's brother Buqing had a mansion to the east known as East Mansion, closer to their birthplace. Also designed by Zhuan Xueren and built during the period 1938–1945, its entry gate and other brick components boast elaborate design.

Yang Tingbao and others, West China Hospital at Sichuan University

Chengdu
1946

Sichuan University is a successor to Sichuan Chinese and Western School that was founded in 1892. The first campus hospital opened in 1914. When Chinese universities and research institutes relocated to the southwestern provinces during the Second Sino-Japanese War, Yang Tingbao was among them. He designed buildings at Sichuan University during this period. His buildings were massive, symmetrically dispositioned, and made of brick and reinforced concrete with red trim and ceramic tile roofs. The hospital follows this design, with a three-story central entry trimmed in red and a Chinese-style hip-gable roof above it, symmetrical side wings, and front corners capped by Chinese-style roofs. Still today the university is entered by a Chinese-style, triple-entry, ceremonial gate of the type known as *pailou*.

Allied Architects, Apartments for Americans, Blocks A and B

Nanjing
1947

Tong Jun of Allied Architects was responsible for designing Blocks A and B of Apartments for Americans in China in the late 1940s. They identify themselves as modern by the front balconies and flat side facades. Interiors had the best heating, plumbing, electricity, and other amenities available in China in the late 1940s.

Liang Sicheng, Xu Jingzhi, Li Huibo, and others, National Central Museum

Nanjing
1948

Preparations for the Nanjing Central Museum began in 1933. When it was completed in 1948, architect Liang Sicheng viewed it as the convergence of traditional Chinese and modern architecture: a steel-framed building of reinforced concrete with bright red pillars, bracket sets, and a ceramic-tile, hipped roof. Liang, who had written the guidelines for its design competition, sought a building that could function as a modern museum while employing Chinese style. The design of University of Michigan graduates Xu Jingzhi (Su Gin-Djih, 1906–1983) and Li Huibo (1909–1950) was selected. The eleventh-century Buddha halls of Huayan Monastery in Datong and Fengguo Monastery in Yi county, Liaoning, were important models for the museum's design.

Kwan, Chu & Yang, Sun Ke Villa

Nanjing
1948

Yang Tingbao designed Sun Ke Villa (Yanhuiguan) for Sun Yat-sen's son, Sun Ke (1891–1973), in 1948, when Yang was part of the firm Kwan, Chu & Yang. It is one of his blatantly modernist buildings, with an interior made almost entirely of glass casement. The villa is evidence that Yang was designing in the modernist idiom even as he was building architecture with Chinese-style big roofs. László Hudec had designed a villa for Sun Ke in Shanghai in 1931.

Xiandai, 1949–1978

ARCHITECTURE OF SOCIALISM

The label *xiandai*, the present age or contemporary, may not be appropriate for an era that ended nearly a half century ago. Yet it is used in Chinese architectural writing about the period 1949–1978, and sometimes extends another decade. Before the end of the period, China reopened to the United States.

The architecture of *xiandai* began with a period of optimism, as new architecture was built for Communist China's first decade. Civic buildings initially remained reliant, sometimes heavily reliant, on Beaux-Arts precedents, even though they included modern systems to circulate air and control climate and often, Chinese ceramic-tile roofs. The middle years of *xiandai* witnessed a schism from China's and other building traditions as the country turned inward, breaking off relations with many nonsocialist nations. Architecture of much of this period was designed to be functional and practical. *Xiandai* ended with optimism at the end of the post–Mao Zedong era and a return to intellectual and financial engagement that had been largely blocked for a quarter of a century. Architects had not forgotten what they had learned or seen before 1949. Those styles and techniques reemerged in buildings such as hotels that would be used by foreigners. By 1978, Chinese students again were studying architecture abroad.

THE 1950s

The 1950s was a decade of tense relations between China and the United States, and US companies and advisers left the country. The Soviet Union dominated China's economic reforms, rebuilding program, and future vision. One feature of Soviet influence was the five-year plan (aimed at major economic development in a five-year period). China's first Five-Year Plan—1953–1957—was coincident with the Korean War. This period was followed by the Great Leap Forward, 1958–1962, also sometimes known as China's second Five-Year Plan. Transformation of the countryside into communes was a major agenda.

A competition that resulted in the Ten Great Buildings (to celebrate the tenth anniversary of the People's Republic of China, and so also known as Anniversary Projects) showcased new, modernist architecture. Most of the buildings stand in Beijing on Chang'an Avenue, extended in the twentieth century to be the longest street in China. Running east–west along the northern border of Tian'anmen Square, it challenges and ultimately counters the north–south line formed by the imperial buildings of the Forbidden City. Constructed around 1958–1959, the buildings are wide structures of three or more stories, but never so high that they are not dominantly horizontal. They have simple, rectangular windows, most of them the same size, framed but otherwise unelaborated. Stadiums from the 1950s also use these kinds of windows. The Chinese modern structures have boxlike central towers, sometimes with pyramidal, tiled roofs at the tops, and sometimes with similar towers at the front corners. They were, in other words, simple and functional, with minimal exterior elaboration and often a roof that identified them as Chinese.

Even beyond Chang'an Avenue, China's most important construction in the 1950s was in Beijing. The millennial-old capital was designed to transform from the last vestiges of an imperial city to the center of the People's Republic. At the Beijing Planning Conference in December 1949, Soviets, architect and architectural historian Liang Sicheng, Paris-trained architect Chen Zhanxiang (Charles) (1916–2001), and others presented proposals for the city, ranging from preservation of the Forbidden City and all remaining gates and pieces of Beijing's city wall to tearing down the Forbidden City and replacing it with new, functional, government offices. The core of the Forbidden City was ultimately preserved and the focus of the transformation was Tian'anmen Square and buildings to its south. Most of the outer wall and gates were destroyed.

In the 1950s, there were eight Chinese universities that offered graduate degrees in architecture. During this decade, architectural design transitioned to the Second Generation, students trained in China by First Generation teachers who had studied abroad.

THE 1960s

The Great Leap Forward did not industrialize China to the extent that was hoped, nor did it modernize agriculture to the measure necessary to eradicate poverty. In 1966 the Great Proletarian Cultural Revolution commenced. Its goals were to eradicate all remnants of capitalism and traditional Chinese society. This revolution had devastating effects on architecture, for any old building—*old* either defined by age or interpreted as representing values of the past—might be destroyed. The subway system began in Beijing in 1969. It would become a world-class metro system that influenced the implementation of similar systems in cities across China by the end of the century.

THE 1970s

New hotels, concert halls, and department stores rose in great numbers beginning in the 1970s. High-rise apartment buildings were constructed in unprecedented numbers. Hundreds of museums were constructed; museums would long continue to be among China's most innovative buildings. China reopened to the United States following the historic visit of US President Richard Nixon (1913–1994) in 1972. Three years later, the official end of the Vietnam War would come. The Cultural Revolution ended with Mao Zedong's death in 1976. By the end of that year his Gang of Four were arrested and the more pragmatic minister Zhou Enlai died. In 1978 Deng Xiaoping chaired the National Congress of the Communist Party. In 1979, China committed to modernizing agriculture, industry, science, and technology, as well as the military.

Liu Shiying, Library and Grand Auditorium of Hunan University

Changsha
1951

The Library and Grand Auditorium of Hunan University were additions to a campus whose history as Yuelu Academy dated to the tenth century and whose oldest buildings were from the Ming dynasty. In 1929, Liu Dunzhen designed a Western-style building for the campus. Most of the modern buildings at Hunan University, however, were designed by Liu Shiying (1893–1973). A year earlier, Liu Shiying had become the director of Suzhou Municipal Engineering, a position from which he oversaw the redesign of Suzhou into a modern city with three main north–south and three east–west streets and canals running through and around the city. In 1934 he moved to Hunan University, where he became director of the Department of Civil Engineering and founded the Architecture Department. He became Dean of Hunan Institute of Technology in 1958 and, later, vice president of Hunan University. Liu also wrote books about Western architecture.

The Library and Grand Auditorium of Hunan University were among forty-two buildings Liu Shiying designed from the 1920s to 1950s. He is best known for modernist designs, but his buildings on the Hunan University campus, including this design, have big roofs broken into parts so that they have gables on both the front and sides.

湖南大學

Yang Tingbao, Peace Hotel

Beijing
1953

Peace Hotel was the first large public building erected in Beijing after the establishment of the People's Republic. It was also Yang Tingbao's first design under the new government. Then head of the Architecture Department of Nanjing University, he designed it with Yang Kuanglin (1891-1971), a University of Michigan graduate and the dean of the School of Engineering and Department of Architecture at St. John's University in Shanghai.

The efficient, minimalist, and modernist Peace Hotel shows yet another aspect of Yang Tingbao's versatility. The structure was designed in response to its site, with its buildings positioned around three existing trees and a well. A wall was added to the remains of an adjacent courtyard-style house to create a plaza on the east side. The main, seven-story building sits along an east–west axis on the north end of the site, while a two-story octagonal ballroom is the focus of the west side. Originally planned as four stories, the soft clay of the site gave way to a seven-story structure whose foundation extended deep enough below ground to support a taller building. Zhou Enlai was impressed with the hotel's functionality and the low budget required to build it. It is an early example of a Chinese hotel with its own parking lot.

Wang Dingzheng, Caoyang New Village

Shanghai
1953

Wang Dingzheng (1913–2014), a graduate of the University of Illinois, proposed the new village (Xincun) housing concept in the 1940s. He introduced Caoyang New Village in an industrial zone of western Shanghai in 1951. Each floor of the complex included three housing units (one of twenty-three square meters and the other two of sixteen square meters), a shared kitchen, and a shared bathroom. Caoyang New Village had a preschool, primary schools, a middle school, gas station, food market, other shopping, public baths, restaurants, medical facilities, a community center, post office, library, movie theater, security office, fire station, housing management office, swimming pool, reserve land, park, factory, and parking.

Eventually more than 200 new villages would house nearly 600,000 workers and their families in a total area of more than 4.7 million square meters. The new villages were divided into clusters that were further divided into neighborhoods. Public transportation was within 600 meters of any part of them.

Clarence Arthur Perry's (1872–1944) idea of the neighborhood unit was influential in creating the new villages. Although Alan Colquhoun's (1921–2012) highly influential essay "The Superblock" would not be published until 1971, builders of new villages in China probably were influenced by similar concepts in Russia. Half of the articles in the 1954 Chinese periodical *Jianzhu xuebao (Architectural Journal)* were about architecture and urban planning in Russia and Eastern Europe. Still, in a 1956 article on Caoyang New Village, Wang Dingzheng criticized himself for turning to a bourgeois concept of neighborhoods rather than to Soviet models. The Baiwanzhuang Residential Area in Beijing and the living quarters of the First Automobile Works (FAW) Factory in Changchun were influenced by Soviet socialist models.

曹杨一村

Hong Qing, People's Grand Hotel

Xi'an
1953

People's Grand Hotel in Xi'an is a magnificent structure by any measure, but extraordinary for 1953. The elegant yet somber building has a domed central section with a two-story entry that recalls art deco. Fleurs-de-lis and other relief recall grand hotels and civic architecture of 1930s China. Yet the building's high central section with long sides and repetitive windows anticipates the style that would become dominant in the 1950s. Hong Qing (1913–2014), the hotel's designer, was chief architect of Northwest Institute of Architectural Design in Xi'an. Built for state and foreign dignitaries, over the past several decades, People's Grand Hotel has come to be recognized as one of the city's most important landmarks.

Wang Fuchen, Palace of Geology

Changchun
1953

This building with a long front facade, a taller central section, repetitive windows, red pillars, white jade balustrades, and big roofs stands on a plaza of green-glazed tiles on a site intended for the Palace of Supreme Harmony of Manchukuo. The building has so many reminiscences of traditional Chinese architecture that it was rumored to have been designed by Liang Sicheng, who did work on buildings at nearby Jilin University. But it was designed by local architect Wang Fuchen. The Palace of Geology includes some modern details, such as geometric patterns rather than owls' tails on the roof ridge ends. Today it is part of Jilin University.

Architect unknown,
First Automobile Works (FAW) Factory

Changchun
1953

Designed by a Soviet team with the participation of architects and students from Tsinghua University, FAW was the first automobile manufacturing plant in China. More than 100 buildings were constructed for the site in the 1950s. Built with Marxist functionality as the primary purpose, Chinese-style ceramic-tile roofs still covered some of them. Before the plant was built, thirty-nine workers visited a Soviet truck factory to learn about operations. China's first truck, the Jiefang (liberation), was built in 1956 and the first car, Hongqi (red flag), was built in 1958. Still in use, and modernized in the half-century since it was first built, FAW is the second-largest state-owned car manufacturing plant in China.

Architect unknown, Beijing University Foreign Housing

Beijing
1954

People's housing was one of the agendas of the Great Leap Forward. The goal was to house large numbers of people in apartments blocks with new facilities, making it possible to remove one-story *hutong* (residences built around courtyards inside lanes and alleys) that had defined residential architecture in Beijing in the nineteenth century and earlier, and replace those neighborhoods with spatially efficient, high-rise apartments.

Concrete apartment blocks of four-to-six stories, sometimes used by work units whose jobs were in nearby or adjacent factories, were typical housing of the late 1950s to early 1960s. Peking University Foreign Housing had exterior articulation in the form of a raised panel above the entrance, but otherwise followed the principles of workers' residential architecture of the period.

Xu Zhong, Sea Creature Garden, Jimei Educational Village

Xiamen
1954

Sea Creature Garden (Aoyuan) at Jimei Educational Village was designed by Xu Zhong (1912–1985) and built through the funding of Tan Kah Kee (Chen Jiageng, 1874–1961). Tan began Jimei Educational Village, which included primary, vocational, and post-secondary schools, on approximately twenty-five acres opposite Xiamen Island in 1913. The complex is among the more than 100 schools Tan established during his lifetime. His two-story residence, a humble structure by comparison to the architecture around it, is on the grounds. His tomb is in Sea Creature Garden, connected to the schools by a winding corridor above the sea. Today the educational buildings are part of Jimei University.

Huang Yulin and Ha Xiongwen, Wenyuan Hall

Shanghai
1954

The H-shaped Wenyuan Hall on the campus of Tongji University, once the campus of a German medical school, is a modernist building. Its designers—Huang Yulin (1927–1953), who had graduated from Tongji, and Ha Xiongwen (1907–1981), who was a Penn alumnus—were trained in Beaux-Arts design. However, in 1943, Richard Paulick (1903–1979), a student of Bauhaus School founder Walter Gropius (1883–1969), taught at Tongji, and by the 1950s other faculty educated in Bauhaus construction also were teaching there. This may explain the look of Wenyuan Hall, an early example of Bauhaus modernism in China. Bauhaus-inspired architecture would not rise again in China until the 1970s.

Dai Nianci, West Building of Beijing Hotel

Beijing
1954

Located on Chang'an Avenue, Beijing Hotel is a complex with multiple buildings constructed between 1900 and 2001. West Building, designed by Dai Nianci (1920–1991) of the Design Institute of the Ministry of Architectural Industry, was added in 1954.

The oldest structure at the Beijing Hotel is the Middle Building, which was built as a restaurant in 1900 and used as a hotel in 1917. East Building was added in 1974. It was the tallest building in Beijing at that time. In 1990, Middle, West, and East buildings were joined, and a building was added west of West Building. Yet another building was added behind Middle Building in 2001. The individual parts present neo-Renaissance, socialist, and modernist architectural styles. The part built in 1954 is known as Block C. Both Nikita Khrushchev (1894–1971) and Richard Nixon stayed in Beijing Hotel, which was for a long time the most distinguished hotel in Beijing.

Zhang Bo, Friendship Hotel

Beijing
1954

Completed in 1954, Friendship Hotel occupies 320,000 square meters. The U-shaped, brick structure surrounds 60,000 square meters of garden. Because of the use of arched windows, lattice patterns that reference Chinese designs, and green-glazed tile that covers the roof eaves of side towers that recall gate towers known as *que*, it has been said that Liang Sicheng proposed the design. In the 1980s, the hotel housed primarily foreign visitors, especially Russians.

Lin Leyi, Capital Theater

Beijing
1955

Capital Theater exemplifies neo-Classicism with the overlay of international Marxist aesthetics and Chinese decorative motifs. The building is symmetrical, with a prominent front of three central bays with double doors flanked by two windowed bays. Side projections toward its front are inspired by *queti* (sparrow's beaks) but here are placed vertically rather than the more typical horizontal use. Lotus patterns are found in the centers of ceilings, in individual lattices of ceilings, and on curtains that frame the emblem of the People's Republic. Concave corners that recall owl's tails project upward rather than outward. The uniform color of the facade is such that the decorative motifs are apparent only close up. Even less visible are Soviet symbols of stars, wheat, and flags. Lin Leyi studied architecture at the Georgia Institute of Technology.

首都剧场
王府井

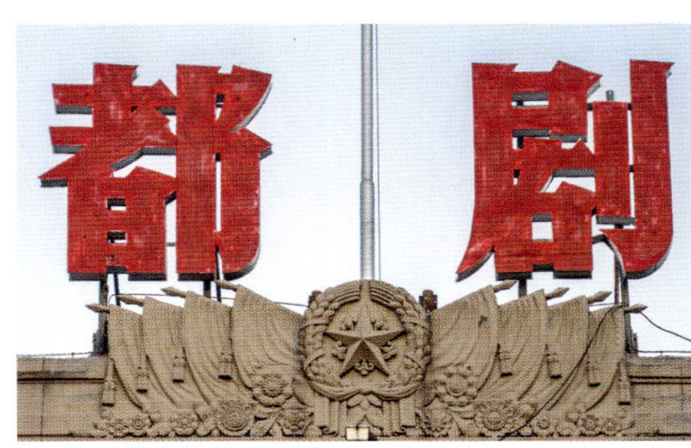
都 剧

Zhang Kaiji, Sanlihe Government Complex

Beijing
1955

Zhang Kaiji (1912–2006), educated in Beaux-Arts design at the National Central University in Nanjing, was a chief architect at the Beijing Institute of Architectural Design and Research. In this capacity he designed some of the most important buildings in Beijing in the 1950s. Sanlihe Government Complex was one of them. The three-story government offices are an example of urban block architecture. The three Chinese-style roofed sections at the center front and corners are references to traditional Chinese architecture, which were rare in buildings of the second half of the 1950s.

Architect unknown, Baiwanzhuang Residential Area

Beijing
1956

Baiwanzhuang was laid out to follow the eight trigrams of the *Yijing (Book of Changes)*. The plan was chosen to negate the negative associations of a cemetery that had once been there. This first New Village in Beijing was built over a period of three years.

Viktor Andreev, Benjamin Chen, and others, Sino-Soviet Friendship Hall

Shanghai
1955

The Sino-Soviet Friendship Hall exemplifies the union of architecture and ideology and the collaboration of architects in the middle of the 1950s. Friendship Hall was an exhibition hall built to showcase the major achievements of the Soviet Union. It stands on the site of a garden designed by a Buddhist monk in imitation of a garden described in the classical Chinese novel *Dream of the Red Chamber*. By 1954, the garden had deteriorated. In ten months, the 131-meter high, 18,300-square-meter building was completed. Viktor Andreev (1905–1988), winner of the 1954 Stalin Prize, who came to China in 1954 to guide design projects, led the team with about seventy Chinese architects, including Benjamin Chen. Their model for Friendship Hall probably was the Main Pavilion of the All-Union Agricultural Exhibition, designed by Yuri Shchuko (1878–1939) and others, which in turn probably was inspired by Russian Beaux-Arts buildings such as the Gate Pavilion to Admiralty designed by Andreyan Zakharov (1761–1811) and built in St. Petersburg between 1810 and 1823.

Lin Leyi and Zhang Zhaoping, Telegraph Service Building

Beijing
1957

Socialist content and style underlay every Chinese building of the 1950s. No manual defined those goals, yet Beijing's Telegraph Service Building exemplifies them. The building is made of reinforced concrete. Its five stories spread horizontally. A tall tower that projects at its center, a clear marker of the symmetry that characterized international modernist architecture in China since the 1930s, had been used in the Soviet Union, and was standard in China in the 1950s. The front of the building's resemblance to a toad with bent side legs gave it the Chinese nickname "toad style." Compared to the Central Broadcasting Building, where Soviet engineers played a larger role in construction, the simpler Telegraph Service Building more recalls designs by Yang Tingbao and other First Generation architects. In June 2017, just short of sixty years in operation, the building closed because so few people had reason to send telegraphs.

Yan Xinghua, Central Broadcasting Building

Beijing
1957

Built the same year the Telegraph Service Center was completed and on the same street, Chang'an Avenue, Central Broadcasting Building may seem to share many features with it. But the Central Broadcasting Building is not "toad style." Instead, it was one of 156 Soviet-aided building projects, and it reflects that contribution. The sharp angles of the three sections of the facade and the octagonal tower at the top call to mind what is often termed Soviet neo-Classicism. In fact, this style is the Soviet descendant of Beaux-Arts training received by Russian architects who studied in Paris in the nineteenth century.

Architecture Design and Research Institute, Beijing Planetarium, Building A

Beijing
1957

The dome of Beijing Planetarium, Building A, designed by Zhang Kaiji, Song Rong (1927–2002), and others of the Architecture Design and Research Institute, identified the structure as a modern planetarium in 1957. The dome, 23.5 meters in diameter, is copper, but the rest of the building is reinforced concrete. The front projection under the prominent, central dome, and long, single-story, symmetrical sides confirm the adaptability of the structural type so prominent in buildings across China from the 1930s to the 1950s: as had been the case in premodern China, this mid-twentieth-century architectural form could be used for functions ranging from hotels to communication buildings to an observatory. While two wings of the observatory house telescopes, sculpture and murals inside feature Chinese legendary and mythological heroes. The first observatory in Beijing was built in the late 1270s by Khubilai Khan (r. 1260–1294). Astronomical instruments from subsequent Chinese dynasties are on display at the observatory.

北京天文館

Liang Sicheng, Monument to the People's Heroes

Beijing
1958

The Monument to the People's Heroes was the first new building constructed south of Tian'anmen Square. The cornerstone was laid on September 30, 1949, at 6:00 p.m., six hours before the official founding of the People's Republic. The decision to place the monument midway between Tian'anmen (Gate) and Zhengyang Gate to the south followed long debate. In 1952, a construction committee was established, with Liang Sicheng as a vice-chair. The obelisk-like structure is made of the highest quality marble and granite. It has Liang's signature Chinese-style roof, reflecting traditional China. The sculpture, executed in a realistic style along the base, illustrates the major events leading up to the founding of the People's Republic—in addition to calligraphy by Mao Zedong and Zhou Enlai.

Beijing Institute of Architectural Design, Great Hall of the People

Beijing
1959

Great Hall of the People, where China's legislature meets, is one of the Ten Great Buildings. Like many of them, it was designed by members of the Beijing Institute of Architectural Design in conjunction with the Beijing Planning Bureau and Ministry of Construction. One of its designers, Zhang Bo (1911–1999), was a student of Liang Sicheng and had an important impact on the redesign of Beijing. He believed this building reflected the goals of Chinese modernism: the excessively long structure had a clear, pillared central space, symmetrical sides that project forward at the ends, uniformly sized windows, and a flat roof. Zhao Dongri (1914–2005), another lead designer of the Great Hall of the People, was a rare Chinese architect who was educated at Waseda University in Japan. He worked for the Japanese in Manchukuo, yet was still able to have a career in China after 1949.

This building, chosen from more than 189 proposals for its design, sits on the west side of the expanded Tian'anmen Square. It is 336 meters across the front, 174 meters deep, and 171,800 square meters total. The excessive size is exhibited by twenty-meter columns across its front, an auditorium with 10,000 seats, and a banquet hall for 5,000. The Museum of the Chinese Revolution and Chinese History, designed by Zhang Kaiji and others, sits opposite it on the eastern side of Tian'anmen Square. Today the museum is known as the National Museum of China.

Beijing Institute of Architectural Design, Minorities Cultural Palace

Beijing
1959

The Minorities Cultural Palace, later known as the Nationalities Cultural Palace, was another building in which Zhang Bo participated and that was completed on Chang'an Avenue for China's tenth anniversary. The central tower, four corner pavilions, and blue-glazed tiles reference traditional Chinese architecture.
One of the Anniversary Projects most similar to the Telegraph Service Building, Minorities Cultural Palace is in toad style, a defining feature of Chinese socialist modernism through the 1950s.

Beijing Institute of Architectural Design, Workers' Stadium

Beijing
1959

The 350,000-square-meter, concrete structure, built to hold more than 65,000 spectators and 1,500 athletes in 300 rooms underground, was another of the Ten Great Buildings. It was used for the World Table Tennis Championship in 1961. The stadium was renovated in the 1980s in anticipation of the Asian Games in 1990 and again before the 2008 Summer Olympics.

Yang Tingbao and Chen Deng'ao, Beijing Railway Station

Beijing
1959

When Beijing Railway Station opened in 1959, it was the largest train station in China. It too was one of the Ten Great Buildings. Yang Tingbao was its lead architect. Placing the towers on either side of the front facade was the idea of Zhou Enlai. Soviets advised in the Stalinist-style aspects of the building that contrasted the Chinese roofs at the top. The 250,000-square-meter station was completed with 2 million workers over a seven-month period. It was built to accommodate 14,000 people in the waiting area and had four escalators. By 1980, as many as 30 million people came through the station annually.

北
BEIJING
京
RAILWAY
站
STATION
进站口
ENTRANCE

Beijing Institute of Architectural Design, National Art Museum

Beijing
1962

The National Art Museum, founded by Mao Zedong, is one of the Ten Great Buildings that was not completed until the early 1960s. Upon its opening it occupied 30,000 square meters. It is one of the last examples of the common 1950s building type with a tall, central tower; portico in front; long, symmetrical sides; standardized windows; and Chinese-style ceramic-tile roofs.

Dai Fudong (1928–2018), Plum Retreat

Wuhan
1963

Mao Zedong visited Plum Retreat (Meiling), his private villa in Wuchang, more than twenty times, once for more than six months. Three single-story buildings are set amid pine and bamboo, as well as plum trees. In Building One, he lived, wrote, conducted national business, and entertained, including dignitaries such as Richard Nixon and Henry Kissinger (b. 1923). Building Two has a lobby and assembly hall and Building Three contained Mao's thirty-meter, six-lane swimming pool.

Mo Bozhi and Zheng Zuliang, Shuangxi Villas

Guangzhou
1965

Mo Bozhi (1915–2003) was an architect who designed to achieve the delicate balance between political ideology, modernism, and the aesthetics of his native region, Southeast China. He is known for two projects in Guangzhou that bridge the Cultural Revolution: Shuangxi Villas, which he completed with Zheng Zuliang (1913–1994) just as the revolution was getting underway, and White Cloud (Baiyun) Hotel of 1976. Shuangxi Villas' flat white facades, latticework, and balustrades and its merging of stone, plaster, glass, open spaces, and plantings disguise the fact that it is organized around two main building units, both approached by a single stone path punctuated by stairs from below. It is almost impossible to see either building in its entirety from any vantage point in the complex. The villas were a retreat for Communist leadership, and they remain guesthouses for which one can make a reservation. Today Mo Bozhi Architects is an award-winning firm, known for its 2021 White Swan Hotel and Conference Center in Taizhou, Zhejiang province.

Beijing Institute of Architectural Design, Qijiayuan Diplomatic Residential Apartments

Beijing
1975

In 1969, Zhou Enlai proposed the Beijing Diplomatic Projects. By 1972, the area included the Beijing International Club and the Friendship Store. The diplomatic residential compounds of Qijiayuan and Jianguomenwai were completed by 1975. All are located along Chang'an Avenue. Zhang Bo worked on the Qijiayuan Diplomatic Residential Apartments. Like him, most of the designers had worked on government projects since the founding of the People's Republic. The buildings reflected the signature Beijing Institute of Architectural Design style of the 1950s, with four-to-six stories along long sections of blocks, sections with high towers, and sometimes, but not always, symmetrical designs. The compounds included green spaces. Interiors had 1970s European amenities and both Chinese and non-Chinese art treasures.

Shanghai Institute of Architectural Design and Research, Shanghai Indoor Stadium

Shanghai
1975

Built by Shanghai's equivalent institute to the Beijing Institute of Architectural Design, the Shanghai Indoor Stadium marked the return of new civic architecture to cities outside Beijing in the mid-1970s. At 33.6 meters high, with 108 windows in vertical rows, it was a fully modern stadium of the 1970s. Yet the azure around the roof and just below it referenced traditional Chinese architecture. The stadium was renovated in 1999 and 2004. It is now used for entertainment events and sporting competitions like table tennis.

Xu Mengpei, Yang Tingbao, and others, Memorial Hall of Chairman Mao

Beijing
1977

The Memorial Hall of Chairman Mao, south of the Monument to the People's Heroes and north of Zhengyang Gate, was the final building in Tian'anmen Square. It runs 220 meters east to west and 280 meters north to south, and its forty granite pillars support a double-eave, glazed, ceramic-tile, flat roof. Within days of Mao Zedong's death, a team from eight provinces came to Beijing to plan this supremely important monument. Once it was decided that the memorial would stand in the square, its height was determined based on the view from existing buildings. The first floor of the interior divides into the North Great Hall on the entrance side, for commemoration, and the South Hall for exit. A marble statue of Mao is in the center. Mao's body is in a crystal coffin draped with the party flag in the central hall. Marble statues of the six leaders of the revolution are on the second floor, together with a movie hall. Materials for the interior were gathered from all thirty provinces.

Dangdai, 1978–2000

REOPENING TO INTERNATIONALISM

More than half of China's current population was born in or after the 1980s. They were raised in a China open to the world and were educated to be world citizens. Compared to the generation of their parents, few have experienced severe poverty. Many have experienced economic prosperity, and many have studied or worked abroad. Whereas political concerns were a, if not the, motivating factor in construction of the previous thirty years, the agenda of architecture in the last twenty-two years of the twentieth century focused on internationalism; buildings were a way to exhibit China's place and participation on a global stage.

The desire for buildings to soar and attract international attention coincided with the understanding that unique designs, assessment of the role of past traditions in contemporary construction, projects bid internationally, and the winning of design competitions by foreign architects symbolized China's intent to have a strong presence in the international economy. Deng Xiaoping, who guided China's post-Mao transition of power and drive toward internationalism through the 1980s, understood the power of architecture to represent China. It was not specifically one of his Four Modernizations (agriculture, industry, defense, and science and technology), and yet it was implicit in Dengist policy that the most challenging designs by the world's most renowned architects proclaimed China's international engagement. Intense construction of museums and hotels underscored this message. Both became important backdrops for proclaiming China's multimillennial past. Bracket sets, shapes of Bronze Age vessels, elements of traditional gardens, and allusions to ideology such as yin-yang and the circle as representing heaven found places in architecture frequented by the increasing numbers of foreigners visiting and living in China. Foreign architects thus sought to implement these shapes and symbols in their projects.

THE 1980s

China's Third Generation, who came of age in the 1980s, are the teachers in the major departments of architecture in China today and architects whose work may be marked by references to traditional styles but always in a modernist or international way. Preservation and renovation of old building complexes and city sections also were major pursuits of architects during the 1980s. In 1986, architects were trained at forty-six Chinese colleges or universities.

THE 1990s

In 1993, the Three Gorges Project, the world's largest hydroelectric dam, began. 1,500 cities and towns would be flooded, and 1.9 million people would be relocated so that the dam could open in 2015. Jiang Zemin became President of the People's Republic of China in 1993 and remained in office for ten years. Under his leadership, China experienced substantial economic growth. In 1997, Hong Kong was returned to China from the United Kingdom. In 1999, Macau was returned from Portugal.

The 1990s brought opportunities for private enterprise and land ownership. In Beijing alone, 3,000 high-rise apartment buildings rose in the 1990s. In 1992, Beijing announced a plan to build 100 department stores of 10,000 square meters or more by the year 2000. More than forty were finished by the mid-1990s. In 1995, 64 percent of China's annual urban construction budget was spent on housing. In 1999, the average floor space in a dwelling was four times what it had been in 1980. Hotels and museums with unprecedented, creative plans rose across China during this decade, as did spectacular shopping malls designed to appeal to the burgeoning consumer culture.

Shenzhen, twenty-seven kilometers from Hong Kong, was a recipient of much of the new construction and in the 1990s was one of the fastest-growing cities in the world. The 1990s also saw the transformation of Pudong, Shanghai's formerly undeveloped district east of the Huangpu River, into a sea of towers.

In 1993, Tsinghua, Tongji, Southeast, and Tianjin universities offered undergraduate degrees in architecture. In 1998, fifty Chinese architects received French government scholarships to study in France.

I. M. Pei,
Fragrant Hill Hotel, Beijing

Beijing
1981

I. M. Pei (1917–2019) described his vision in architecture as "modern Chinese vernacular." Vernacular for him was represented by a city like Suzhou, whose white walls of garden architecture are used in Fragrant Hill Hotel. Not wanting to compete with the architecture near the Forbidden City, Pei selected a site in Beijing's Fragrant Hills Park for this hotel commission and decided not to build a skyscraper. The hotel is built around a central atrium that receives natural light from the skylight above, with white-washed walls and gray tile common in Southeast China and with winding wings that reference the mazes of gardens and private homes of the region. Two preexisting 800-year-old ginkgo trees and huge rocks from Yunnan are incorporated into the design. The hotel is considered Pei's statement about modernism in a Chinese vernacular context.

Born in Guangzhou, Pei immigrated to the United States in 1935, enrolled at the University of Pennsylvania, and then transferred to MIT, where he found the Beaux-Arts curriculum similar to that at Penn, and went on to Harvard, where he studied Bauhaus architecture with Walter Gropius. In 1955 he established Pei & Associates, which later became Pei Partnership Architects, the firm where his sons work today. Pei had already designed John F. Kennedy Library and the East Building of the National Gallery when he was asked to design this hotel. He won the Pritzker Prize in 1983.

Beijing Institute of Architectural Design, Liulichang

Beijing
1982

Liuli is the Chinese name for a type of glazed ceramic tile that was used in important architecture, including palaces, official mansions, and monastery buildings. Liulichang, a factory that produced *liuli* tiles, operated in this Beijing neighborhood from the mid-thirteenth through mid-seventeenth centuries and gave its name to the area. Beginning in the mid-seventeenth century, merchants began to sell old books, antiques, and items used for painting and calligraphy here. Rongbaozhai (Glorious Treasures Studio), founded in 1672, still sells calligraphy and painting. The area fell into disuse in the twentieth century. In 1982 a several-block area of Liulichang was restored to its nineteenth-century appearance. The active shopping area, known as the place in Beijing to find antiques and rare books, became a model for similar shopping arcades across China.

010-87283986

Beckett International, Great Wall Hotel

Beijing
1983

Great Wall Hotel was Beijing's first joint-venture, five-star hotel. Located at the heart of the city's commercial and financial districts, it represents China's frenzy for large-scale modernism in commercial architecture of the early 1980s. A curtain wall—a nonstructural facade of a building that protects it from weather—was used here for the first time in China.

Qi Kang, Wuyi Mountain Villa

Mount Wuyi
1983

Mount Wuyi in Fujian province contains the largest subtropical rain forest in China. It is also a repository of inscriptions carved in stone. Qi Kang (b. 1931), a professor at Southeast University and major force in architectural design of the 1980s, built Wuyi Mountain Villa onto a shallow mountain slope with the goal of merging its architecture with the landscape. The overhanging eaves, white stucco walls, and brown wooden frames reflect a vernacular style of Southeast China.

Xiang Xinran, Yellow Crane Tower

Wuhan
1985

The 51.4-meter, five-story Yellow Crane Tower on Snake Hill dominates the view of Wuhan. Named after its roof eaves, which curve upward like the wings of a crane, its history traces to 223 CE when the original tower was used as a military watch tower. Beginning in the seventh century, the tower was a common subject in Chinese painting and poetry. Damaged and rebuilt twelve times and destroyed in 1884, the tower was reconstructed about one kilometer from its original site and the grounds of the historic tower were renovated as an important Chinese preservation project in the 1980s. The current structure is based on the Qing dynasty version. 100,000 glazed, ceramic tiles are used on the exterior. Yellow Crane Tower is symmetrical on every side.

The tower was never the tallest building in China, nor the most extraordinary. It is an example of a structure whose supreme importance is grounded in legend and literature. Daoist immortals are said to have arrived here on yellow cranes. Some say the Daoist immortal Lü Dongbin ascended to heaven from here. The most popular legend associated with the tower relates that a Daoist was offered kindnesses from the son of a wine shop owner and drew a crane on his wall that would dance upon request. Ten years later, the Daoist ascended to the heavens on this crane. Tang poets Li Bai (701–762) and Bai Juyi (772–846) wrote poems about Yellow Crane Tower.

Dai Nianci and Fu Xiurong, Queli Guest House

Qufu
1985

Dai Nianci and Fu Xiurong designed the Queli Guest House in Qufu, the hometown of Confucius, in 1985, when Dai was China's deputy minister of construction. Located next to China's most important Confucian temple, Dai chose elements that accurately reflected the country's oldest architecture: a roof with simple, overhanging eaves for the gateway in front of the main building, a roof with hips and gables and two sets of roof eaves above the main structure, and single-story guest rooms at the sides. Whereas the ceramic-tile roofs reflect ancient China, the building materials and white exterior confirm the building's modernism. The plantings and patterns on stone are in the manner of details at the Confucian Temple. The style of the complex has been called neo-National.

Chen Jihong, Square Pagoda Garden

Shanghai
1986

The 42.5-meter, tenth-to-eleventh-century Square Pagoda was built at Xingshengjiao Monastery in Songjiang, today a district of Shanghai. The pagoda's screen wall, relics, and bridges have survived nearly 1,000 years. Square Pagoda Garden and other monastery buildings came later. The pagoda and gardens are considered models of preservation and redesign of an ancient space for contemporary visitors.

Qi Kang, Memorial of Meiyuan New Village

Nanjing
1987

This memorial recognizes the site where peace talks between the Communists and the Guomindang took place in 1946–1947. Entered by a vine-covered wall, in 1954 this former residence of Zhou Enlai and other Communist leaders became a museum of the Chinese Revolution. Except for a brief period in the early 1960s, it was closed until 1977. Qi Kang's renovations date to 1987. He also designed the Memorial Museum to Victims of the Nanjing Massacre in Nanjing.

Architect unknown, Huqingyutang Museum of Traditional Chinese Medicine

Hangzhou
1988

Huqingyutang began in 1874 as a pharmacy of the official Hu Xueyuan (1823–1885). Born in Anhui and apprenticed to a banker, Hu would eventually own his own bank, as well as have interests in shipping and real estate. In 1884 he went bankrupt and died the next year. A century later, in 1988, his medicine hall became the 4,000-square-meter Museum of Traditional Chinese Medicine, the only museum of tradition medicine on this scale in China. The museum includes an exhibition hall, a medicine preparation hall, a clinic using traditional Chinese medicine, a restaurant, and a shop.

Lu Jiwei, Kempinski Hotel

Beijing
1992

In 1897, wine merchant Berthold Kempinski (1843–1910) founded what today is Europe's oldest luxury hotel chain. In 1992, architect Lu Jiwei of Tongji University received the commission to design a Kempinski Hotel in Beijing. Located in the financial and diplomatic hub of Beijing during the frenzy of tourist-hotel construction in the early 1990s, the 526-room Kempinski Hotel was the first five-star, joint-venture Sino-European hotel in the city. It was renovated in 2019. One might view the front facade as referencing a centrally posed tall section with symmetrically posed sides, and with uniformly sized windows that appear as varied because of the use of color. One also observes the marble bridge whose balustrade posts recall those of the approaches to buildings of the Forbidden City and the prominent use of circles and squares. But the hotel was first and foremost intended to provide luxury for the most prominent and influential international visitors to Beijing in the last decade of the twentieth century.

Shanghai Construction Group, Oriental Pearl Radio and Television Tower

Shanghai
1994

Oriental Pearl Radio and Television Tower stands in Pudong, across the Huangpu River from the Bund. When construction began in 1991, its signaled that Pudong was to become not only the financial center of Shanghai but also the hub of unique, dramatic, contemporary architecture. The 468-meter structure was the tallest building in Shanghai until 2007. Supported on a pyramidal base, the tower comprises three large, five small, and three decorative spheres. When light shines on them, they look like pearls. The largest, just below the vertical midpoint, has a diameter of fifty meters. The second largest, with a diameter of forty-five meters, is directly above it. Three cylinders, each nine meters in diameter, join them. The tower has fifteen observation levels, a revolving restaurant, a museum of Shanghai history, other exhibition halls, shopping, and a hotel. The pinnacle is a 118-meter antenna. The tower weighs 120,000 tons.

Xing Tonghe, Shanghai Museum

Shanghai
1996

The Shanghai Museum was established in 1952. It reopened in the current building in People's Square in 1996. Architect Xing Tonghe (b. 1939) took inspiration for the shape of the museum from a bronze vessel in its collection. The combination of circle at the top and square on the ground references a passage in a ritual text of the first millennium BCE that says Heaven is round and Earth is square.

Liu Li, Henderson Center

Beijing
1996

Henderson (Hengji) Center is a nineteen-story structure at its highest point. This central tower with four clocks, short posts with bracket-set-like braces, pyramidal roof, and finial with rings that seem to reference the *chatra* at the pinnacle of a pagoda recall architecture in China's cities in the 1930s, Chang'an Avenue's Ten Great Buildings, and premodern timber-frame elements. A mall is on the lower four floors, and offices and one- to three-bedroom apartments are above. The building's residential section contains a two-floor clubhouse reminiscent of construction in early-twentieth-century Shanghai for foreigners. In 1996 Henderson Center was a harbinger of towering mixed-use construction that is common in China's cities today.

北京站街

Qi Kang, Henan Museum

Zhengzhou
1997

Designed by Qi Kang, this museum with 78,840 square meters of interior space houses 130,000 of Henan province's most important objects as well as natural history displays. The building is designed with a central, circular opening that receives the maximum natural light at noon. Groups of stars identified in ancient times to represent the four directions and the center are inlaid in the upper parts of this opening. Light blue transparent windows symbolize the belief that the waters of the Yellow River come from the heavens. Interior decoration makes reference to traditional Chinese features such as bracket sets.

Arte Charpentier, Shanghai Grand Theatre

Shanghai
1998

A graduate of the University of Paris and L'École Nationale Supérieure des Beaux-Arts, Jean-Marie Charpentier (1939–2010) taught architecture for a year in Cambodia, founded Arte Charpentier, and in 1984 became one of the first Europeans to establish a practice in China. The 1,800-seat Shanghai Grand Theatre in People's Square, has a 3,700-square meter stage. It was made with 7,000 tons of steel, much of which is used for the roof and some for the cables from which the glass curtain walls are suspended. The glass facade makes it possible for anyone on the street to see the audience, restaurants, and shops. Charpentier turned to the frequently employed symbols of square like the Earth for the structure and round like the heavens for the roof. Arte Charpentier completed the Shanxi Grand Theater in the city of Taiyuan in 2012.

Skidmore, Owings & Merrill, Jin Mao Tower

Shanghai
1999

Soaring 420.5 meters with eighty-eight stories plus five in its spire, Jin Mao Tower was the tallest building in China and third-tallest in the world when it was completed. Its design was led by architect Adrian Smith (b. 1944) of Skidmore, Owings & Merrill. Shanghai Institute of Architectural Design and Research collaborated on its engineering. The tower's diminishing perimeter from base to roof and the shape of its spire are inspired by the profile of a Chinese pagoda. Two elevators transport passengers the entire height of the building in forty-five seconds. The eighty-eight floors divide into sixteen segments, each one-eighth shorter than the height of the one below it. The exterior curtain wall is made of glass, stainless steel, aluminum, and granite and is crisscrossed by complex latticework cladding made of aluminum alloy pipes. At night, the spire lights up a sixty-meter long, 1.2-meter-wide skywalk on the 88th floor. The observation deck holds more than 1,000 people.

Jin Mao Tower rests on steel piles sunken 83.5 meters into the ground. The structure is designed to withstand an earthquake of 7 on the Richter scale and typhoon winds up to 200 kilometers per hour. The tower is built around an octagonal concrete shear wall core surrounded by two pairs of eight exterior steel columns that absorb shock. The swimming pool on the fifty-seventh floor is designed to act as a passive damper, an anti-earthquake device.

Pei Partnership Architects, Bank of China Headquarters

Beijing
1999

China's majority-state-owned bank is the fourth-largest bank in the world. Founded in 1912 to replace the Da (Great) Qing Government Bank, it is China's second oldest bank; Bank of Communication was founded in 1908. In 2020, Bank of China was the fourth-largest bank in the world in terms of total assets. Pei's design drew on the efficiency of the corner structure, which had utilized space from wall to wall across the corner in Chinese cities since the 1930s.

Dangdangdai, 2000–Present

CONTEMPORARY GLOBAL ARCHITECTURE

China's twenty-first century can be called the age of Supertall and Megatall. Upon completion, a building often was the tallest structure on Earth. No matter its height, buildings were international in every sense of the word. Architects from every continent competed to design in China and buildings were usually indistinguishable from those anywhere in the world. Occasionally, a reference to a traditional Chinese feature such as a bracket set or an auspicious number would be incorporated. Chinese firms designed outside China as often as domestically. Museums continued to offer unparalleled opportunities for architectural creativity.

Cutting-edge technology is apparent in every detail of a twenty-first century Chinese building. Transparent layers of glass replace the need for single-layer, opaque glass of facades, new materials that simulate traditional ones such as glazed tiles are created, and steel is manipulated so that exterior curvature can occur in any direction and stationary buildings with twists and curves appear to move. Twenty-first century architecture also has achieved sustainability in new and creative ways. Rain water and waste water have been recycled for ponds and pools inside architectural complexes. In new construction, sense of place and vernacular identity can be accomplished with recycled local materials from stone to wood to bamboo and references to the past are possible through green spaces that follow patterns of traditional Chinese gardens. Complexes with more than 10,000 employees are built with car-free zones and green corridors, yet easy movement is possible throughout. Challenges of past construction—whether height, materials, never-before seen spaces, or a climate from desert to ice-covered—have disappeared. Enormous airports have been constructed, old airports have been renovated and expanded, and new terminals stand in towns where air travel was not possible until the twenty-first century.

THE 2000s

China's growth into the second-largest global economy occurred in this decade. The number of state-owned enterprises dropped from 10 billion in the 1990s to 300,000 by the early 2000s.

In 2000, China was admitted into the World Trade Organization. In 2001, the World Planning Schools Congress was held at Tongji University. In 2003, China launched its first manned spacecraft. The Chinese premier, Wen Jiabao (b. 1942), addressed the Japanese Parliament in 2007, the first time since the founding of the People's Republic. Between 2004 and 2008, Chinese household consumption increased by close to 10 percent per year. After a decade of preparation, China hosted the Olympics in 2008. In 2008, nearly all urban dwellers in China had air conditioning, a color TV, at least one cell phone, and a washing machine. 60 percent had a home computer, and more than 50 percent had a microwave. According to government reports, 4 percent of people in urban China lived below the poverty line. China's Fourth Generation of architects came of age in this decade.

THE 2010s

The 2010s has been called China's Decade of Technology. China became the largest exporter of goods, the largest producer of steel, a huge producer of passenger cars, and ever-increasing purchaser of cars. According to government statistics, nearly all children across China received at least nine years of education. 40 percent of China's students were enrolled in undergraduate programs and 36 percent were in graduate programs. The average size of a city apartment rose to sixty-five square meters for a family of three; most units were equipped with air conditioning, color TVs, washing machines and other large appliances, and computers. China worked to reduce pollution and add green spaces to its cities. Sustainability, sense of place, or recognition of the vernacular identity of a location, and creativity, whether in sinuous steel, newly conceived materials, ventilation, acoustics, or height, guided design and were primary agendas of construction. Challenges to past achievements in height, use of materials, or never-before-seen spaces were commonplace.

THE 2020s

In 2020, China's GNI was 24.08 trillion PPP dollars, compared to 12.33 trillion in 2010. The city Shenzhen and the architecture of international mega enterprises including Alibaba, Tencent, and Huawei, have played large roles in this unprecedented urban growth. China's Belt and Road Initiative has accomplished for China in Eurasia what the Silk Roads never could. Entering the third decade of the twenty-first century, China is a major producer of steel and the largest car maker in the world.

Amateur Architecture Studio, Wenzheng College Library, Suzhou University

Suzhou
2000

Designed by Wang Shu (b. 1963) and Lu Wenyu (b. 1966) of Hangzhou-based Amateur Architecture Studio, Wenzheng College Library draws on Suzhou's water, gardens, and white walls, for which the city is famous. Its sharp angles, built in brick, cement, steel, and glass, reference the site's mountainous backdrop. Three stories, and appearing in some exterior views as two stories, are aboveground; the rest of the building is below ground. The south-facing structure comprises four parts, each a pavilion-like reference to a scholar's studio. One pavilion hovers above the water. The design for a place to read poetry and philosophy is positioned to suggest the balance of human and nature.

AZL Architects, Nanjing University Graduate Student Dormitory

Nanjing
2000

Verticality, horizontality, creativity, bold color, and functionality mark this early building by Zhang Lei (b. 1964), an architect who is committed to adapting his buildings to the environment for which he creates. Bringing the vision of a rising-star architect to a student dormitory signals China's twenty-first-century investment in a future that expects to go far beyond the bare necessities for every aspect of life.

Foster + Partners, Jiushi Headquarters

Shanghai
2001

Jiushi Headquarters is British firm Foster + Partners' first building in China. It is also the first building in Shanghai to use triple-skin, ventilated, glazed glass for maximum daylight. Three evenly positioned terraces punctuate the forty-story structure; the highest of them is the base of a six-story garden. A multi-floor arcade at ground level, along the Huangpu River, recalls architecture of nearly a century earlier.

Foster + Partners, led by Norman Foster (b. 1935), followed Jiushi Headquarters with several buildings in China, including Bund Finance Center in Shanghai in 2017, Citic Bank Headquarters in Hangzhou in 2017, Hongqiao Vantone Sunnyworld Center in Shanghai in 2018, and Shanghai Bund Riverside in 2020. Foster + Partners won a competition in 2020 to design the Alibaba headquarters in Shanghai.

上海久事

Multiple architects, Commune by the Great Wall

Beijing
2002

In 2002, twelve architects were offered the opportunity to design eleven residences and one clubhouse on an eight-square-kilometer space near a section of the Great Wall in the Shuiguan Mountains at Badaling. Each villa was to cost approximately USD 1 million. Power couple Pan Shiyi (b. 1963) and Zhang Xin (b. 1965) of SOHO China sponsored the project. Gary Chang's (b. 1962) Suitcase House, which has underground bathrooms, and Kengo Kuma's (b. 1954) Bamboo Wall House are among the best-known villas.

竹屋7
Bamboo Wall 7

John Portman, Tomorrow Square

Shanghai
2003

Atlanta-based, Georgia Tech-trained John Portman (1924–2017) appeared unexpectedly on the scene in China with his Shanghai Centre of 1990, one of the first post-Mao Zedong projects designed by an American architect. Like Shanghai Centre, Tomorrow Square aroused the kind of enthusiasm Portman's Merchandise Mart and Hyatt Regency had brought to Atlanta some forty years earlier. Located a short distance from Shanghai Centre, Tomorrow Square is a sixty-three-story, 285-meter, concrete tower that turns 45-degrees at the thirty-seventh floor. Known for hotels with open interiors, the architect-developer also built the three-tower, mixed-use Yintai Center in Beijing, which opened in 2008.

Wang Lu, Tiantai Museum

Tiantai
2003

Tiantai Museum is an early project of Wang Lu (b. 1963), a professor at Tsinghua University. Wang sought to use local materials, to integrate the site into the mountain, Tiantai, for which this part of Southeast China is known, as well as to design specifically for the range of objects to be exhibited. He accomplished this with three sets of spaces: the outermost, along the road; a second, which opens to the river, holds the permanent collection; and the third is used for temporary shows. Exhibition spaces are of different sizes. Those for sculpture and other three-dimensional objects are large and open; those for display of two-dimensional objects such as paintings are smaller and have load-bearing walls.

MADA s.p.a.m., Father's House

Lantian
2003

Ma Qingyun (b. 1965), founding partner of MADA s.p.a.m., designed this house for his father in his native town of Lantian, one of the thirteen administrative ccunties of Xi'an known for its exceptional scenery. Located between mountains and a river, the house uses local materials. The design is distinguished by its many surfaces and textures and by its natural colors of materials. Human-made materials such as concrete are used to a minimum.

Yung Ho Chang, Hebei Education Publishing House

Shijiazhuang
2005

Yung Ho Chang (b. 1956), following a stint at MIT, established his practice, Atelier Feichang Jianzhu, in China in 1993. Chang's design for the Hebei Education Publishing House in Shijiazhuang occupies the top three floors of a 16,800-square-meter, twelve-story structure. Below the floors used for publishing are two towers linked by an open space that contain offices, a museum, a restaurant, and an indoor basketball court.

GMP, Nanning International Convention and Exhibition Center

Nanning
2005

GMP won an international competition to design this as a Guangxi regional convention and exhibition center. The 90,000-square-meter Nanning Center is built in a park outside the center of Nanning. Visitors can experience the nearby lake and look down on the city. A seventy-meter-high, translucent tower designed to look like an unfolding blossom is the hub of the complex. The prize-winning German firm went on to build Maritime Museum in Shanghai in 2009, renovate and extend the National Museum of China in Beijing in 2011, followed by Nanjing Financial City I, completed in 2017, Chinese Traditional Culture Museum in Beijing, completed in 2022, and hotels, schools, railroad stations, hospitals, industrial parks, and other conventional centers across China.

Kohn Pedersen Fox, CNOOC Headquarters

Beijing
2006

The CNOOC (China Natural Offshore Oil Corporation) Headquarters is one of many high-rise towers built by the multinational firm Kohn Pedersen Fox (KPF) in China. Located at a major crossroads along the Second Ring Road in Beijing's eastern Dongcheng district, the structure of more than 1 million square meters is meant to evoke images of an oil tanker's bow and oil derrick and the ground below it. The floor-to-ceiling sun-filled atrium has differently shaped sky gardens on each side.

Zhu Pei, Blur Hotel

Beijing
2006

Blur Hotel is the outcome of the renovation of a large government building into a hotel next to the west gate of the Forbidden City. Zhu Pei's (b. 1962) primary goal was to transform the private, closed space into open public space. Mindful of courtyard-style housing in the neighborhood, he designed vertical rather than horizontal courtyards. Blur Hotel's semitransparent facade resembles a Chinese lantern that brings light into the building on every floor.

Amateur Architecture Studio, Ceramic House

Jinhua
2006

Ceramic House is a 100-square-meter café-house. Hangzhou-based Wang Shu, dean of the School of Architecture of the Chinese Academy of Art, and winner of the 2012 Pritzker Prize, said the inspiration for it was a Song dynasty inkstone. Wang envisioned someone drinking coffee in this café during the intense wind and rain that characterize Jinhua in Zhejiang province.

I. M. Pei, Suzhou Museum

Suzhou
2006

I. M. Pei's goals for a museum in China's city of famous painters, elite literate culture, and most acclaimed gardens were twofold: to capture the local, vernacular tradition of white plaster walls and gray roof tiles; and to make it possible to change ambiance but not experience when walking to the adjacent nineteenth-century residence and sixteenth-century Garden of the Unsuccessful Politician. The structure offers much more. The sharp lines and angles, use of glass, and bridges provide individual and interconnected sections around a central water court and gazebo. The focus on water recognizes that it also is a vital component in Suzhou, through whose streets canals flow. As in a Suzhou garden, the museum viewer can stand in the same place and with a slight turn have a totally different view. This allows for an overarching symmetry around irregular spaces that reference a Chinese garden. The Suzhou Museum can be described as Pei's contemporary imaging of a Chinese sixteenth-century city of luxury.

Paul Andreu, National Centre for the Performing Arts

Beijing
2007

French architect Paul Andreu's (1938–2018) National Centre for the Performing Arts is in one of the most prominent places in Beijing. Known for the designs of Charles de Gaulle and Orly airports, Andreu designed this building to rise from a lake adjacent to the Great Hall of the People on the west side of Tian'anmen Square. To enter, one takes a transparent, sixty-meter underpass. The dome is covered in 18,000 pieces of oxidized titanium. The elliptical structure is forty meters high and has a surface area of 149,500 square meters. Because no building in Tian'anmen Square was to stand taller than the Great Hall of the People, there was incentive for the structure to continue underground. Glass allows light in during the day; its interior lights up Beijing during night performances. The building's opera house, concert hall, and theater seat a total of 5,500. Opera is performed at the center, an ellipse inside the ellipse.

Herzog & de Meuron, National Stadium

Beijing
2007

Swiss graduates of ETH in Zurich and joint winners of the 2001 Pritzker Prize, Jacques Herzog (b. 1950) and Pierre de Meuron (b. 1950) are known for their creativity, innovative solutions, and range of modernism. They are also known for using a material to its fullest extent. A stadium in the shape of a bird's nest (earning it that nickname), yet inspired by a Chinese ceramic vessel, exemplifies these traits. Construction began with the concrete foundation into which the steel frame of the stadium was installed.

The curved steel for the frame was made in Shanghai and brought to Beijing for assembly and welding. Floors, walls, and beams were poured on-site. Initially the specifications called for a retractable roof. This was abandoned because support for it in such a large structure would have required a perhaps dangerously heavy support system. Related to concerns about mass, the intended 91,000 capacity was reduced by about 10,000. Twenty-four enormous columns, each weighing about 1,000 tons, were still needed to support the interior "vessel," which does not stand on flat ground. The entrance is higher than the rest of the stadium to alleviate stress. The modular turf grass field is 7,811 square meters. Used for the opening and closing ceremonies of the 2008 Summer Olympics, the National Stadium seats 80,000 with capacity for another 10,000 inside the building. Li Xinggang, of China Architecture Design and Research Group, participated, Stefan Marbach was lead architect, Ai Weiwei (b. 1957) contributed as artist and curator, and Arup was the engineering firm.

Arata Isozaki, Central Academy of Fine Arts

Beijing
2008

Founded as an art college in the late nineteenth century and becoming a university in the 1990s, the Central Academy was relocated to Wangfujing, Beijing, in 2001. RIBA Gold Medal- and Pritzker Prize-winner Isozaki (1931–2022) completed the design in 2008. Described as sensuous, boomerang-like, and reptilian, four levels of this slate-covered building are above ground and two are underground. The exterior is a strong contrast to the smooth, primarily white interior where light and shadow are used so that gallery space can accommodate contemporary as well as ancient art.

Amateur Architecture Studio, Ningbo Museum

Ningbo
2008

Millions of reused, multi-sized bricks and ceramic tiles from destroyed local buildings, and concrete cast in bamboo molds are used in the 30,000-square-meter building. The human-made materials combine with allusions to water and mountains in this well-known building by Amateur Architecture Studio principal Wang Shu. The lower facade rises vertically from the ground, while its upper walls tilt like mountains. Ningbo History Museum won the Lu Ban Prize in 2009, the top architecture prize in China.

Kohn Pedersen Fox, Shanghai World Financial Center

Shanghai
2008

The 101-floor, 492-meter Shanghai World Financial Center was the second-tallest structure in the world when it was completed in 2008. Made of steel and reinforced concrete, the building has diagonal braces in the frame that make the height possible. The trapezoidal-shaped opening at the top, which reduces wind stress, is one of the building's distinguishing features and gives it its nickname, Bottle Opener. Shanghai World Financial Center is an example of the expensive, mixed-use, architecturally challenging buildings that rose in Chinese cities in the early twenty-first century. Its first floor is a mall; its upper floors contain offices, conference rooms, and hotel rooms; and observation decks are on floors 94, 97, and 100. Together with Shanghai Tower and Jin Mao Tower, it is part of a trio that defines the Pudong landscape.

Steven Holl, Linked Hybrid

Beijing
2009

Each of the eight towers of Steven Holl's (b. 1947) 220,000-square-meter Linked Hybrid complex has windows on every side. Interaction among buildings is achieved not only by linking them with bridges, but also by connections at the ground level and below ground. The glass and steel bridges, twenty to sixty meters long, are mounted on bearings so that they can move independently during an earthquake. A variety of functions—commercial, residential, educational, and recreational—exist at ground level. While similar mixes have been part of high-rise construction in China for nearly a century, this project includes the added feature of a central pool. In a city of megatall architecture, the lower buildings occupying large amounts of space make a profound statement on the landscape. Linked Hybrid has 644 apartments, and each floor has four 74- to 150-square-meter apartments with views on two sides. The buildings use geothermal heating and cooling systems. Wastewater is recycled to irrigate the lawns. Red, blue, yellow, and green are used as on the undersurfaces of bridges and around some windows.

Henn Architekten, Automotive Expo Museum

Beijing
2009

Henn Architects was founded in 1979 by Günter Henn (b. 1947), who had been educated in Munich, Berlin, and Zurich. The firm has offices in Munich, Berlin, Beijing, and, most recently, Shanghai. The son of an architect, Henn's son now runs the practice. In 2003, Henn won the competition for what became the first building at Beijing's Automotive Museum. Because of roads and marketing potential, the ground floor became two buildings with an open passageway between. An elliptical opening that widens to the top joins the exhibition areas of the larger building. Henn's Haikou Towers, begun in 2016, will rise 428 meters and be the tallest buildings on Hainan Island.

Architect unknown, Guangdong Maritime Silk Road Museum

Yangjiang
2009

The Maritime Silk Road connected China's southeastern ports with the Arabian Peninsula by way of southern India. This museum on Hailing Island, Yangjiang, in Guangdong province, stands on the wreck of a tenth-century wooden ship named South Sea (Nanhai) No. 1. Found in 1987, the ship contained more than 60,000 objects, including thousands of examples of ceramic wares from Jingdezhen in Jiangxi, Dehua ware from Fujian, and Longquan ware from Zhejiang. Gold and silver objects and copper coins also were recovered. To encompass and recover the wreck, a bottomless steel container was placed above it. The container was then driven into the seabed with concrete weights and then closed underneath with steel sheets so that it could be raised. The 19,409-square-meter museum is inside a water tank with the same water quality, temperature, and environment as those of the wreck. Archaeologists also work inside this space. Four small, elliptical halls surround the large, central hall containing South Sea No. 1. The major items from the excavations were cleaned of the natural deposits from the sea and are on display.

Information Based Architecture, Canton Tower

Guangzhou
2009

The 604-meter Canton Tower lights up the city of Guangzhou. It was the tallest tower in China when it opened in time for the 2010 Asian Games. The tower's hyperbolic shape is created by two ellipses, one at the base and a second 450 meters above ground. The tower narrows to twenty-two meters near its center, a silhouette sometimes compared to a small-waisted woman. It breaks at interior intervals, each with its own central ceiling to let in light, with the significant feature of emitting its own light at night. The potential for earthquakes was important in the design. In addition to its role as a television and radio tower, Canton Tower functions as a center of entertainment and observation.

Hassell, Alibaba Headquarters

Hangzhou
2009

About 20 percent of Alibaba's 100,000 employees work in this 150,000-square-meter complex. The architects were asked to follow three principles—connectivity, clarity, and community—on small and large scales. The Alibaba campus is designed around a central courtyard with clusters of four- to seven-story buildings. From any structure, one can see across the courtyard to all other building complexes.

Bridges and roof terraces where small groups can meet enhance the goal of community. Sustainability is addressed with horizontal screens that reduce the heat of the sun and vertical windows on both sides of the building for cross ventilation. Patterns found in Hangzhou gardens are used on these screens, thus recognizing the city's significant past in a place intended to lead China into the future.

Alibaba

Ge Xiurun, Baiheliang Underwater Museum

Chongqing
2009

The underwater museum is built around inscriptions that record the rise and fall of the Yangzi River. The earliest inscription dates to 763. It is one of 166 in the museum, 105 of which record the water level measured by the location of eighteen engraved-stone fishes placed to make those measurements as accurate as possible. Displays also include two statues of the bodhisattva Guanyin and a white crane (*baihe*), which gives the museum its name. The museum is forty meters below ground, entered by a ninety-one-meter escalator followed by a 146-meter corridor. Construction with non-pressure containers took seven years. In 2012, the museum won a design award from the Architectural Academy of China, and in 2013 it won the outstanding design award from China's Ministry of Education.

Rocco Design Architects, Guangdong Museum

Guangzhou
2010

Rocco won the competition for this new museum for Guangdong province in 2004, to be located in the new center of Guangzhou along with the opera house and library. It offers 41,000 square-meters of space in four stories above ground and another 15,000 square-meters below ground. Natural light comes from a large, central skylight. The form has been compared to the Chinese ivory puzzle ball whose exterior layers can be pulled off, to a lacquer box, jade bowl, and bronze tank. One enters the multi-layered box-shaped space along a diagonal passageway, in the manner of entering a Chinese tomb. Aluminum panels, fritted glass, and GRC (glass-fiber reinforced concrete) panels of different depths are carved into the exterior, presenting different degrees of transparency that offer varying relations between interior and exterior.

Zaha Hadid, Opera House

Guangzhou
2010

Winner of the Pritzker Prize, Stirling Prize, and Royal Gold Medal of the Royal Institute of British Architects, Hadid's work is characterized by unprecedented and unorthodox forms that express movement and speed. In April 2002, Zaha Hadid (1950–2016) won the international competition for an opera house in Guangzhou. Her submission was named "double pebble," reflecting the idea of two rocks washed away by the Pearl River. It is also said to be inspired by the washing away of river valleys through erosion. An 1,800-seat auditorium and 400-seat hall made it the third largest performance hall in China, after Beijing's National Centre for the Performing Arts and Shanghai Grand Theatre. The concrete structure sits inside an exposed granite and glass-clad steel frame in a newly developed culture center of Guangzhou.

He Jingtang, China Pavilion

Shanghai
2010

The China Pavilion was built for Expo 2010 Shanghai as the largest national display building at a cost of more than 200 million dollars. In 2012, it was converted into the China Art Museum, whose galleries, some of them underground and others to the side, occupy 45,000 square meters. Nicknamed Oriental Crown, the China Pavilion rises sixty-three meters. Its shape is inspired by a bracket set, as is its color: bracket sets traditionally were painted in China's most auspicious color, vermilion. Architect He Jingtang (b. 1938) uses seven shades of red. The ends of beams are decorated like their counterparts 1,000 years ago.

Architectural Design and Research Institute, Tsinghua University, Century Hall

Beijing
2010

The 31,720-square-meter hall with 11,230.5 meters underground was built to celebrate Tsinghua University's centennial. It is used for conventions, performances, and exhibitions. Isosceles triangles take shape on the outer wall of the circular theater so that light and shadow project into the hall in the triangular intervening spaces. Although Century Hall has no dome, the circular shape references Murphy and Dana's domed Auditorium that had been built ninety years earlier.

新清華學堂

AUBE, Guiyang International Conference and Exhibition Center

Guiyang
2011

AUBE Conception SARL d'Architecture was founded in Paris in 1997. The next year it opened an office in Shenzhen. Guiyang's conference and exhibition Center is the largest multifunctional center in southwestern China. Designed by AUBE, it was built by Zhongtian Urban Development Group. Occupying an area of a million square meters, a complex of this size signaled Guiyang's ambitions to become a major commercial city. AUBE Conception went on to design International Conference and Exhibition Center in Shaoxing, Zhejiang province, and Shenzhen World Exhibition and Convention Center in 2019. All three massive, mixed-space complexes are distinguished by enormous interior spaces, huge land mass, steel, and sensitivity to the environment.

HYATT REGENCY
中天金融集团

Hiroshi Oshima, Concert Hall

Xuzhou
2011

As the birthplace of the founding emperor of the Han dynasty (206 BCE–220 CE), Xuzhou has a history of important architecture beginning with Han royal tombs. The Xuzhou Concert Hall designed by Hiroshi Oshima (b. 1957) joins these tombs as one of the city's most important structures. The shape of this building on the bank of Yulong Lake is inspired by the eight-petaled crepe myrtle plant, the city flower of Xuzhou. The 13,000-square-meter complex includes the 28.9-meter, eight-story, 10,530-square-meter music hall, an outdoor performance shell, and an entrance plaza. Three floors are underground. The Concert Hall is supported with tubular steel. Aluminum sheets of the facade use double-hyperbolic honeycomb-core sandwich panels designed to withstand wind.

Kengo Kuma, Zhi Museum

Xinjin
2011

Kengo Kuma (b. 1954), a professor at Tokyo National University, is known for using and juxtaposing irregular shapes, angles, and tilts that challenge space and view. He does this using local materials in the museum in Xinjin, Sichuan province, which sits at the foot of a mountain dedicated to philosopher Laozi. Exhibitions focus on Daoism. The exterior is made of local tiles that are hung by wire to suggest weightlessness. Wire suspension allows for dark spaces blocked by tile and other spaces that receive light. Irregularly placed tiles and tilting facades suggest natural imbalance even though the museum is of two stories with level floors.

HWCD Associates, Bamboo Courtyard Teahouse

Yangzhou
2012

Sun Wei of Harmony World Consulting & Design (HWCD) designed this teahouse with asymmetrical, cubic, brick rooms joined by louvered bamboo corridors and sun-deflecting brises soleils. Located on a lake, it appears to float on water. Vertical and horizontal bamboo create corridors along the perimeter. Bamboo also is used to define courtyards, each with a view of the lake. In some rooms, bamboo drops from the ceiling like a curtain.

Office for Metropolitan Architecture, CCTV Headquarters

Beijing
2012

Known for his creativity, Rem Koolhaas (b. 1944), founder of Office for Metropolitan Architecture (OMA), designed CCTV Headquarters in Beijing. It stands 234 meters with fifty-one stories. Due to a fire the year after completion, the tower officially opened in 2013. Nicknamed Big Pants for its shape of two towers joined by a saddle at the top, the structure comprises six horizontal and six vertical strips that yield 473,000 square meters of floor space.

CCTV

Tianjin University Research Institute of Architectural Design & Urban Planning, Liuzhou Fantastic Stones Museum

Liuzhou
2012

The city of Liuzhou in central Guangxi province is located at the confluence of the Liu and Luoqing rivers, waterways into which the Hongshui River flows. Stones from this river are believed to be magical and are prized for use in jewelry and other ornaments. In 2012, a museum for these stones was built. Faced with Liuzhou stones, its shape fits into the landscape in a manner as natural as rockery. The 12,392.8-square-meter space, 22.1 meters at its highest point, was conceived in 2009. More than 100 types of stones are among the more than 1,000 on exhibition.

Zaha Hadid,
Galaxy Soho Building

Beijing
2012

With eighteen floors and 332,857 square meters of largely commercial and office space, as well as entertainment and dining, Galaxy Soho exemplifies Hadid's ability to create curvilinear structures expressing motion. Four glass-topped, ovoid buildings, each of different dimensions, are joined by curving passageways. A large central canyon and other courtyards on different levels are Hadid's interpretation of the Chinese courtyard. The exterior is aluminum and stone. The interior is glass, terrazzo, stainless steel, and glass-reinforced gypsum.

GALAXYSOHO

Yung Ho Chang, Vertical Glass House

Shanghai
2013

Yung Ho Chang received an honorable mention for this 1991 submission to the Shinkenchiku Residential Design Competition hosted by *Japan Architect*. In 2013, the four-story, forty-square-meter structure with concrete walls was built as a permanent pavilion for the West Bund Biennale of Architecture and Contemporary Art in Shanghai. The concrete walls were poured with rough formwork on the exterior and smooth board inside, offering a contrast in texture and surface from the inside out. A central steel post and steel beams divide the interior into four, and each quarter of the house is intended for a different activity. All the floors are made of seven-centimeter-thick composite tempered glass slabs, and light transmits through the glass. The Vertical Glass House is operated by the West Bund Biennale as an architectural exhibition as well as a guest house for visiting artists and architects.

Steven Holl, Sifang Art Museum

Nanjing
2013

The upper gallery of this museum offers changing views to the outside at each opening, including a view of Nanjing in the distance. Sifang Museum is one of twenty-four China International Practical Exhibition of Architecture projects planned for the site. The courtyard reused bricks from courtyard-style houses of Nanjing. Local bamboo was used to form the concrete on the exterior. Geothermal heating and cooling systems and recycled water were used.

Li Xinggang, Jixi Museum

Jixi
2013

The design for the 10,000-square-meter Jixi Museum, in Anhui, was made after surveying the landscape and studying local architecture, especially the white-washed, flat-sided, gray-roofed residential construction in Huizhou. The museum's continuous roof is based on mountains and waters that undulate in the region. The roof reflects the name of the town and its museum, *ji* meaning *twisted hemp thread* and *xi* meaning *small mountain stream*, reflecting the two streams that converge into a pool at the main entrance.
The complex includes courtyards and pathways that were built to preserve as many trees as possible. Local materials were used to the extent possible in the construction.

Multiple architects, Value Factory (Float Glass Factory)

Shenzhen
2013

Established in 1980 as China's first Special Economic Zone, Shenzhen has risen to one of the most competitive global financial centers with one of the highest number of billionaires in the world, and a population of more than 20 million. The history of the Guangdong Float Glass Factory very much reflects the transformation of the city. The factory opened in 1987 with the most advanced technology, Italian machinery, and US manufacturing processes. By 2009 it was the world's largest manufacturer of standard curtain-wall glass, producing 3 million truckloads a year. At that time, however, the neighborhood had become too expensive for the factory to maintain itself there.

In 2013, the factory was transformed into Value Factory, a contemporary space used as the headquarters of the Bi-City Biennale of Urbanism/Architecture, whose curator was Dutch architectural historian and editor Ole Bouman (b. 1960). The central staircase of the transformed space is described as following the interior of the Guggenheim Museum in New York. The new space is part of the revaluation of so much of Shenzhen's architecture of the late twentieth century, as the city takes on its increasingly important role in twenty-first-century China.

JDP Architects, Guangzhou Circle

Guangzhou
2013

Joseph di Pasquale (b. 1968) of JDP Architects in Milan seeks to design innovative interpretations that do not abandon cultural identity for a contemporary urban environment. He uses hybrid modular systems in his designs. The 85,000-square-meter Guangzhou Circle embodies these principles. The structure stands at 138 meters and has thirty-three floors. Its circular shape references the circle as the Chinese symbol of the heavens. A central opening, forty-eight meters in diameter, gives it the nickname, Donut. The patterns on the facade are influenced by decoration on circular jade disks of China's first and second millennia BCE. In this way, di Pasquale has established Guangzhou Circle's identity as Chinese. Yet it also follows the Italian Renaissance concept of "squaring the circle," for the rooms behind the circle are squared-off conventionally. Guangzhou Circle is the headquarters of Guangdong Hongda Xinye Group and home of Guangdong Plastic Exchange, the world's largest stock exchange for raw plastic material.

MAD Architects, China Wood Sculpture Museum

Harbin
2013

This 13,000-square-meter structure, 200 meters in length, is covered by steel plates that reflect light. The walls twist and turn in a fashion popular in the early twenty-first century. Skylights bring in natural light. The interior is divided into two exhibition halls. Ma Yansong (b. 1975) worked under Peter Eisenman and Zaha Hadid before founding MAD Architects in 2004.

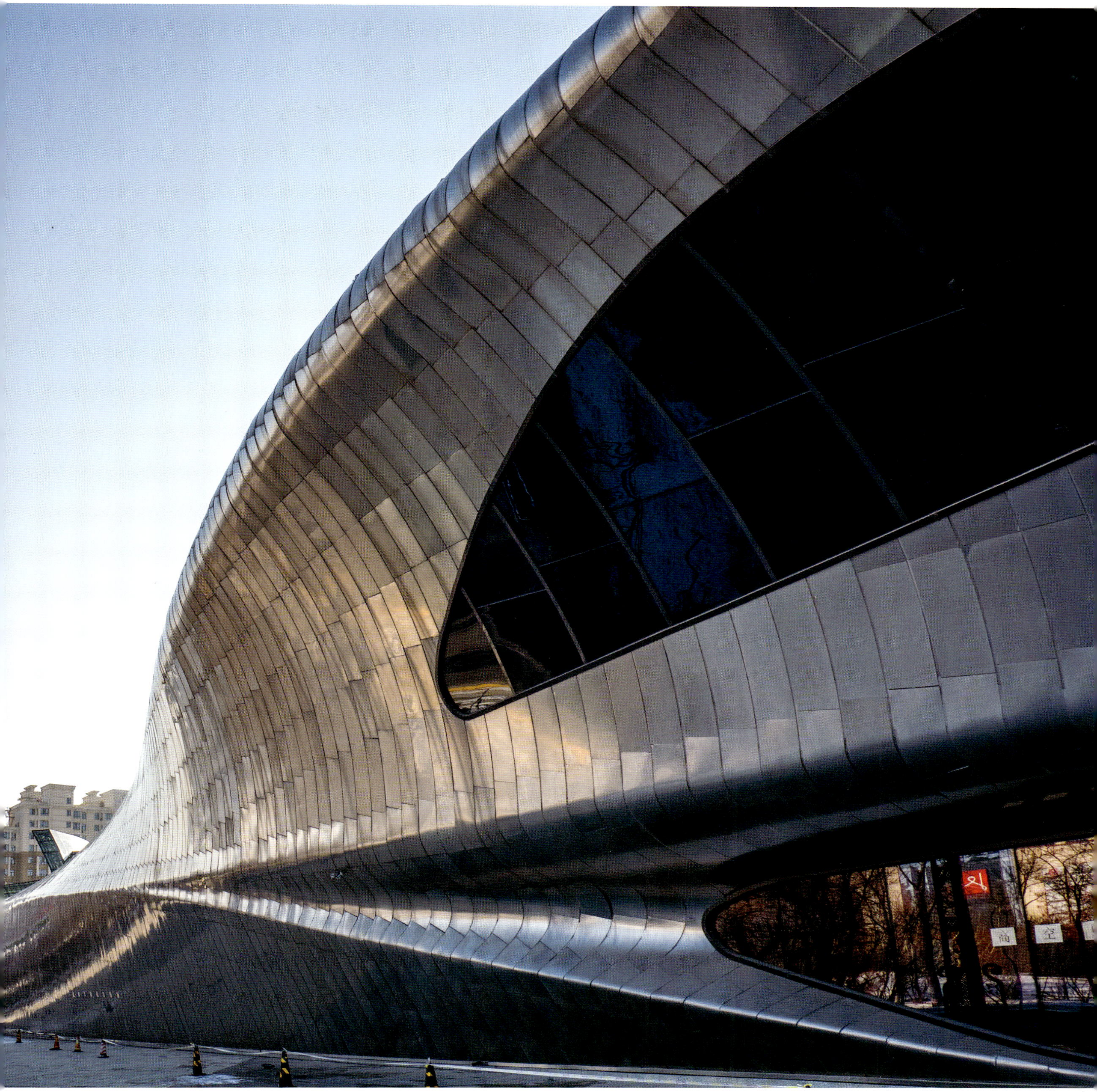

Architect unknown, New Century Global Mall

Chengdu
2013

This 1.7-million-square-meter mall has the largest usable floor area of any building in the world. It includes nearly 400,000 square meters of shopping, a 5,000-square-meter water park, two hotels, food court, skating rink, IMAX theater, museum, and university.

GLOBAL CENTER

Paul Andreu, Jinan Grand Theater

Jinan
2013

Jinan Grand Theater is five oval, domed structures raised on a stone platform and surrounded by parkland in the center of the capital of Shandong province. The exteriors of the three main, domed buildings are covered with opaque metal cladding with glazed strips along their central lines. The changes in surface lines of the domes are not visible from the interior. The theater is entered through the central hall.

Arata Isozaki, Himalayas Art Museum

Shanghai
2013

Isozaki intended this 150,000-square-meter museum to be a twenty-first-century sculptural masterpiece. The central entrance is intended to reference a porous forest with grottoes through which the visitor can wander. The Himalayas Center is a mixed-use building including a five-star hotel, shopping mall, theater, and offices in addition to the art museum.

Liu Yichun, Atelier Deshaus, Long Museum

Shanghai
2014

Funded by art collectors Liu Yiqian (b. 1963) and Wang Wei (b. 1963), Long (Dragon) Museum on the West Bund is one of three museums the couple now owns in China to showcase their premodern and modern Chinese and non-Chinese art. Tongji University-educated Liu Yichun (b. 1969) sought to integrate Chinese ideology into this design. Concrete on the front facade references pillars and bracket sets above them. Windows are positioned to bring views of nature to the interior. The long concrete corridors on the first and second floors reference covered arcades in traditional Chinese architecture, but in fact were built in response to a coal-conveying platform. The 33,000-square-meter Long Museum houses 16,000 square meters of exhibition space. The four-floor main building is vaulted.

Stufish Entertainment Architects, Han Show Theater

Wuhan
2014

The design of the theater is based on a paper lantern. Its surface is decorated with 18,000 ceremonial rings, or *bi*, objects that were the entitlement of royalty in the Zhou (1050–256 BCE) and Han (202 BCE–220 CE) dynasties. The theater has movable seats, a pool, and one of the world's largest movable LED screens.

Dong Yugan, Red Brick Art Museum

Beijing
2014

The 20,000-square-meter site with nearly 10,000 square meters of exhibition space for contemporary art was designed by Beijing University professor Dong Yuguan (b. 1967). The main structure is a two-story, building with red brick walls, floors, and stairs and concrete seating, walkways, and ceilings. It includes exhibition rooms, a public area, and a shop. The central area is beneath a skylight and has balconies overlooking it.

AZL Architects, Wanjing Garden Chapel

Nanjing
2014

Wanjing Garden Chapel is a rare Christian space designed in the twenty-first century. Only 200 square meters, the steel and wood building presents a stark structure whose interior is even starker due to the use of only white. Long, narrow, unpainted strips of wood on the exterior are held in place at the top and bottom by metal. The nearly square floor plan is deceiving. The building is entered on either of two corners, each beneath a roof pinnacle, but the chapel is accessed at a third corner. A long, narrow skylight follows the roof slope, bringing natural light above the altar at one end wall of the interior. A central, octagonal space is created by corridors and walls.

Gensler, Shanghai Tower

Shanghai
2015

Shanghai Tower stands at 632 meters and 128 stories. Floors 84–110 are used as a hotel. When first built, it had the world's fastest elevators. Shanghai Tower is made of nine cylindrical buildings, one on top of the other. Each level has its own atrium. The facade consists of two transparent layers, the outer one twisting as it rises. The double layer means that neither layer needs to use the opaque glass that is necessary in single-layer facades. Shanghai Tower was built with sustainability as an important aspect of every stage. It recycles both rainwater and wastewater.

MAD Architects, Opera House

Harbin
2015

Ma Yansong's architecture follows the design principle promulgated in China known as "mountain-water city." The goal is to build as nature builds, but outside nature. It is employed here at the Harbin Opera House where two sinuous structures rise out of a wetlands neighborhood along the Songhua River and merge in a three-dimensional walking path through an urban plaza. The larger building has a 1,600-seat theater, clad in wood from Heilongjiang, and its smaller theater seats 400 and has a soundproof glass wall. The 79,000-square-meter, modulating structure is made of white aluminum that can merge with the snow that covers one of China's coldest cities in China's coldest province, Heilongjiang. A transparent glass wall along the lobby and glass portions of the roof, some curved and others with sharp edges, further follow the patterns of ice and snow while bringing the maximum amount of natural light to the interior. Harbin Opera House received Acero's Building of the Year award in 2016.

Chen Wei,
Bao'en Monastery Pagoda

Nanjing
2015

The Porcelain Pagoda of Bao'en Monastery was commissioned in 1412 and completed in 1431. The nearly 100-meter, nine-story, octagonal structure could be ascended by a spiral staircase of 184 steps at the center. Every exterior porcelain tile was made in triplicate for easy replacement if one were damaged. European travelers Johan Nieuhof (1618–1672) in 1665, who had seen the pagoda, and Johann Fischer von Erlach (1656–1723) in 1721, who had not been to China, illustrated it in books that were translated into additional European languages and widely disseminated in Europe. It was the tallest pagoda in China until it was destroyed during the Taiping Rebellion in the 1850s. In 2010, a Chinese philanthropist donated 1 billion RMB to pay for the pagoda's reconstruction. Chen Wei was the lead architect. A new material was invented for its exterior with the goal of shining as the structure did in the fifteenth century. A museum stands on the excavation site in front of the pagoda.

Gerkan, Marg & Partners, Guanghualu SOHO 2

Beijing
2015

This sixty-three-meter, fourteen-story, 100,000-square-meter, five-building, curving complex, with 84,000 square meters of offices and another 19,000 square meters for shorter-term use, is in the middle of an active neighborhood. Passageways and overpasses provide interconnections among the buildings.

The curvature and flow extend to the entire exterior, walls as well as roofs, portions of which include gardens. Natural light easily enters the three lowest floors. Above them, light is provided by vertical louvers in the glass portions of the facade.

光华路
SOHO²

Coop Himmelb(l)au, Museum of Contemporary Art and Planning Exhibition

Shenzhen
2016

The Museum of Contemporary Art and Planning Exhibition is part of the master plan for the Futian Cultural District, the new urban center of Shenzhen. It combines the Museum of Contemporary Art (MOCA) and the Planning Exhibition (PE), the latter for architectural exhibitions. For efficiency, the two spaces share an entrance, outer walls, and roof. The entrance is known as "cloud" because its walls and ceiling curve amorphously. A transparent facade and internal lighting allow a view into the entrance and transitional areas and views out onto the city. Cloud contains a cafeteria and shops in addition to the entrance. Cloud, both museums, and access to them are enclosed in an outer layer of stone louvers and a climate shield of insulated glass. The structure is intended to be energy efficient, using primarily solar and geothermal energy and with maximum lighting coming through the roof. In 2012, Coop Himmelb(l)au designed the International Conference Center in Dalian.

THAD, Tsinghua University Library, Phase Four

Beijing
2016

Tshinghua University Library is a building with a century-long history whose four parts reflect the architectural designs of leading architects of their day. Initially designed by Henry Murphy and completed in 1919, the second phase of construction was designed by Yang Tingbao in the 1930s, and the third construction phase was designed by Guan Zhaoye (1929-2022) in the 1980s. Part four comprises a four-story wall in front of a three-story, transparent facade, joined by openings in the wall. The inner space enclosed by this wall is a collection-reading area inside a high-tech structure. All four parts are interconnected.

Kohn Pedersen Fox, Ping An Finance Center

Shenzhen
2017

KPF, known for extremely tall buildings, is the design firm for the 118-floor, 599-meter skyscraper with 495,520 square meters of floor space built for Ping An Insurance Company. The top two stories are used for observation. The stainless steel of the facade weighs approximately 1,700 metric tons. The cost of construction was about USD 1.5 billion.

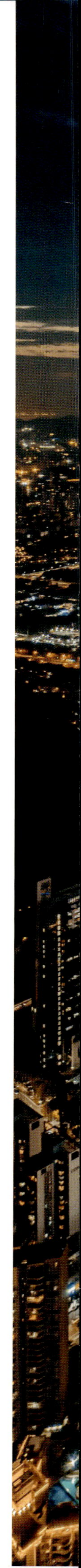

ICBC

Neri&Hu Design and Research Office, Tsingpu Retreat

Yangzhou
2017

Tsingpu Retreat is a 4,200-square-meter, twenty-room boutique hotel near Slender West Lake. Designed by Neri&Hu Design and Research Office, led by Lyndon Neri (b. 1965) and Rossana Hu (b. 1968), the hotel is built around courtyards. Paths connect its buildings. Irregular paths have to be followed to find a room, lending privacy to fundamentally courtyard-style architecture. Bricks from torn-down local buildings were reused in the retreat's construction. The varied patterns of recycled brick reflect and emit different amounts of light. Sited on water, no part of the building is more than two stories.

MAD Architects, Chaoyang Park Plaza

Beijing
2017

Ten buildings rise as natural, amorphous forms in this 220,000 square-meter complex in Beijing's central business district. Adjacent to a park, the mixed-use design intends to extend the park into the city and human-made space into the natural environment. The curvilinear roofs of the tallest buildings span the plaza like mountains and rockery, and the vertical fins on their glass facades offer energy-efficient ventilation and filtration. A pond at the base of the towers not only reflects the buildings but also cools the air inside them. Chaoyang Park Plaza was awarded the LEED Gold Certification by the US Green Building Council for the integration of nature and green technology.

NBBJ, Tencent Seafront Towers

Shenzhen
2018

Located in Shenzhen's High-Tech Industrial Park, the Tencent Seafront Towers, nicknamed Synergy Towers, were designed by NBBJ for one of China's fastest-growing companies. The location, structure, and concept of the building are appropriate for the 12,000 employees who work there. The two-tower structure that joins at three sections expresses the goal of interconnectivity among employees. The new industrial park, which is intended to compete with California's Silicon Valley, is isolated and self-contained like an island. To the extent possible, the industrial park is car free, with green corridors for pedestrians, public transportation, or electric cars. Compared to many older buildings, Tencent Seafront Towers' energy use and carbon emissions are reduced by 40 percent. The towers are positioned to take maximum advantage of wind ventilation while minimizing direct exposure to the sun. The curtain wall controls sun glare while a shading system controls the amount of sun exposure.

Tencent 腾讯

Zaha Hadid, Leeza SOHO

Beijing
2019

Leeza SOHO brings immediate attention and activity to Fengtai, a business district south of Beijing. Forty-five stories and 172,800 square-meters, the tower divides into two halves enclosed by a shell. The space between the two parts is a 194.2-meter atrium, the tallest in the world when built, which rotates through the building to the top. The atrium brings in natural light as well as providing ventilation and air filtration. Sky bridges connect the two halves on levels 13, 24, 35, and 45. Both halves shade the atrium. A double-insulated, glass curtain wall on each floor provides narrow ventilating registers for air control. Leeza SOHO meets the LEED Gold certification and US Green Building Council standards for energy efficiency. Its green roof has a photovoltaic array to collect solar energy, and it has spaces for 2,680 bicycles and charging spaces for electric cars.

丽泽SOHO

Kohn Pedersen Fox, CITIC Tower (China Zun)

Beijing
2019

Soaring 528 meters, the 109-story CITIC Tower was the tallest building in Beijing, the fourth tallest in China, and the eighth tallest in the world upon completion. Its shape is inspired by a *zun*, a second-millennium BCE vase-like, wine vessel that has a flattened, rectangular front and back, curved sides, and a wide mouth at the top. The tower is seventy-eight meters wide at the base, fifty-four meters near the center, and sixty-nine meters at the top. Aluminum is an important building material in this structure that was conceived with great attention to its location in an earthquake-prone zone. Low curtain walls and glass-roofed entries provide a human scale on the first above-ground story. The tower is next to OMA's CCTV Headquarters, hubs of a commercial center in Beijing.

Wang Shu, Lin'an Museum

Hangzhou
2020

Lin'an Museum spans a commercial block. Local brick, shale, rammed earth, gravel, mud, wood, and tiles combine with steel, concrete, and plaster in this complex sited with the Gongchen Mountains to the east and a lake to the south. Overhanging roofs and conjoined roofs reference the vernacular tradition of southeastern China. Entered on the south, the most auspicious direction in premodern construction, halls of varying shapes and sizes are woven into the uneven terrain. Bridges and walkways connect some of them. The combination of buildings function as a museum, with bamboo hallways to guide the direction of visitors and intramural metal security panels in the galleries.

Foster + Partners, Datong Art Museum

Datong
2021

Datong and the environs is the location of some of China's most important excavations and rock-carved art of the fourth and fifth centuries and some of China's most important extant buildings of the eleventh and twelfth centuries. In the twenty-first century, museums were built for those artifacts and impressive preservation joined urban renewal around the architecture. The 32,000-square-meter Art Museum brings a venue for contemporary art to a contemporary cultural plaza in Shanxi province's northern city. Conceived as a set of interconnected pyramids that rise from below ground level, where art works cannot receive natural light, yet energy can be conserved, diagonal lines dominate interior space, as well. The underground gallery space is joined by a media library, lecture and conference rooms, and a place for archives. Light enters from the roofs.

Kohn Pedersen Fox, Huamu Lot 10

Shanghai
2022

According to design principal Jeffrey A. Kenoff, Huamu Lot 10 "seeks to flip the equation of a tower, which typically engages an iconic top, and instead amplify a cantilevered gallery at the mid-point of a tower." Light from these "sky galleries" (Tower 1 stands 179.9 meters with thirty-six floors) thus emits across Shanghai rather than upward. This mixed-use complex also includes a museum. Glass curtain-wall facades bring the maximum amount of natural light into the building and allow for the maximum view to the outside. Each facade is shaded to reduce solar heat while still allowing daylight to enter. Insulated glass is used. Rainwater collected on the roofs is recycled for irrigation and cooling. Fins provide shade and protect against sun glare. Drainage is directed straight downward to avoid exterior staining.

Arup, Beijing Municipal Institute of City Planning & Design, and CCTN Architect Design Company, Shougang Industrial Heritage Park

Beijing
2022

Covering an area of 8.6 square kilometers, Shougang Park is on the site of a steel mill that in 1919 produced 10 million tons of iron and steel. In 2008, Beijing promulgated a plan to transform this area into greenspace that would signal the greening of the city. It has become the model for the transformation of former industrial areas to ecologically sensitive spaces. In 2022, the park was the official entrance to the Winter Olympics. Shougang Industrial Park includes a 94,000-square-meter exhibition hall. Driverless vehicles have been tested here in demonstration areas. This site exemplifies the merging of past and present, which is fundamental to construction of the entire modern period discussed in this book.

秀池北路
<西 秀池北路
W XIUCHI BEILU

Further Reading

Suggested Further Reading on Chinese Architecture, 1840-2020

Bickers, Robert and Isabella Jackson. *Treaty Ports in Modern China: Law, Land and Power.* London: Routledge, 2016.

Clark, Anthony. *China Gothic: The Bishop of Beijing and His Cathedral.* Seattle: University of Washington Press, 2019.

Cody, Jeffrey. *Building in China: Henry K. Murphy's "Adaptive Architecture."* Hong Kong and Seattle: University of Washington Press, 2001.

Cody, Jeffrey, Nancy Steinhardt, and Tony Atkin. *Chinese Architecture and the Beaux-Arts.* Honolulu and Hong Kong: University of Hawaii and Hong Kong University Presses, 2011.

Denison, Edward. *Architecture and the Landscape of Modernity in China before 1949.* London and New York: Routledge, 2017.

Denison, Edward and Guang Yu Ren. *Building Shanghai: The Story of China's Gateway.* Chichester: John Wiley and Sons, 2006.

______. *Modernism in China.* Chichester: John Wiley and Sons, Ltd, 2008.

______. *Ultra-Modernism: Architecture and Modernity in Manchuria.* Hong Kong: Hong Kong University Press, 2016.

Dodington, Spencer and Charles Lagrange. *Shanghai Art Deco Master.* Hong Kong: Earnshaw, 2014.

Elder, Chris. *China's Treaty Ports: Half Love and Half Hate.* Hong Kong, Oxford, and New York: Oxford University Press, 1999.

Erh, Tung-ch'iang, Martha Lund Smalley, and Tess Johnston. *Hallowed Halls: Protestant Colleges in Old China.* Hong Kong: Old China Hand Press, 1998.

Farris, Johnathan. *Enclave to Urbanity: Canton, Foreigners, and Architecture from the Late Eighteenth to Early Twentieth Centuries.* Hong Kong: Hong Kong University Press, 2016.

Fujimori Terunobu and Wan Tan. *Zen chōsa higashi Ajiakindai notoshi to kenchiku* (Comprehensive study of modern East Asian urban planning and architecture). Tokyo: Chikuma shobō, 1996.

Hardie, Kris, Peter Rowe, et al. *Beautified China: The Architectural Revolution.* Belgium: Lannoo, 2019.

Interior Designer. *Chinese Architecture Today.* Basel: Birkhauser, 2016.

Hibbard, Peter. *The Bund.* Hong Kong: Odyssey, 2008.

Hofmann, Michael. *Deutsche Kolonialarchitektur in China und der Südsee.* Petersberg: Michael Imhof, 2016.

Jacobson, Claire. *New Museums in China.* New York: Princeton Architectural Press, 2014.

Jiatu Wenhua. *Dangdai Zhongguo jianzhu* (Contemporary Chinese architecture). 3 vols. Nanjing: Jiangsu kexue chubanshe, 2014.

Johnston, Tess. *Far from Home: Western Architecture in China's Northern Treaty Ports.* Hong Kong: Old China Hand Press, 1996.

______. *Frenchtown Shanghai: Western Architecture in Shanghai's Old French Concession.* Hong Kong: Old China Hand Press, 2000.

______. *God and Country: Western Religious Architecture in Old China.* Hong Kong: Old China Hand Press, 1996.

______. *The Last Colonies: Western Architecture in China's Southern Treaty Ports.* Hong Kong: Old China Hand Press, 1997.

______. *A Last Look: Western Architecture in Old Shanghai.* Hong Kong: Old China Hand Press, 1993.

Lai Delin, Wu Jiang, and Xu Subin, eds. *Zhongguo jindai jianzhu shi* (History of modern Chinese architecture). 5 vols. Beijing: China Architecture and Building Press, 2016.

Liu Xianjue. *Zhongguo jinxiandai jianzhu yishu* (The art of modern architecture in China). Wuhan: Xinhua shudian, 2004.

_____. *Zhongguo jinxiandai jianzhu yu chengshi* (Architecture and cities of modern China). Wuhan: Huazhong Keji Daxue chubanshe, 2018.

Lu Hong and Xia Qing. *A Panorama of the Historic Architecture in Tianjin.* Beijing: China Architecture and Building Press, 2007.

Nield, Robert. *The China Coast.* Hong Kong: Joint Publishing, 2010.

______. *China's Foreign Places: The Foreign Presence in China in the Treaty Ports Era, 1840-1943.* Hong Kong: Hong Kong University Press, 2015.

Roskam, Cole. *Designing Reform: Architecture in the People's Republic of China, 1970-1992.* New Haven: Yale University Press, 2021.

______. *Improvised City: Architecture and Governance in Shanghai, 1834-1937.* Seattle: University of Washington Press, 2019.

Sewell, Bill. *Constructing Empire: The Japanese in Changchun, 1905-45.* Vancouver and Toronto: University of British Columbia Press, 2019.

Shanghai Municipal Tourism Administration. *Tour of Shanghai's Historical Architecture.* Zhengzhou: Henan Meishu chubanshe, 1994.

Steinhardt, Nancy S. *Chinese Architecture: A History.* Princeton: Princeton University Press, 2019.

Sweeten, Alan. *China's Old Churches.* Leiden and Boston: Brill, 2020.

Valentin, Nilda. *The Influence of Western Architecture in China.* Rome: Gangemi Editore, 2017.

Victor, Laura and Victor Zatsepine, eds. *Harbin to Hanoi: The Colonial Built Environment in Asia, 1840-1940.* Hong Kong: Hong Kong University Press, 2013.

Warner, Torsten. *Deutsche Architektur in China /German Architecture in China.* Berlin: Ernst and Son, 1994.

Warr, Anne. *Shanghai Architecture.* Sydney: Watermark Press, 2007.

Wright, Arnold. *Twentieth-Century Impressions of Hong-kong, Shanghai, and Other Treaty Ports of China.* London and Shanghai: Lloyds, 1908.

Xue, Charlie Q. L. *Building a Revolution: Chinese Architecture since 1980.* Hong Kong: Hong Kong University Press, 2006.

Xue, Charlie Qiuli and Yingchun Li, "Importing American Architecture to China: The Practice of John Portman & Associates in Shanghai," *Journal of Architecture* 13, 3 (2008): 317-333.

Yu, Shuishan. *Chang'an Avenue and the Modernization of Chinese Architecture.* Seattle: University of Washington Press, 2012.

Zhang Fuhe. *Beijing jindai jianzhushi* (History of modern Chinese architecture in Beijing). Beijing: Tsinghua University Press, 2004.

Zheng Yangwen. *Sinicizing Christianity*. Leiden: Brill, 2017.

Zhu Jianfei. *Architecture of Modern China: A Historical Critique*. London and New York: Routledge, 2009.

Zou Denong. *Zhongguo jianzhu 60 nian, 1949-2009: Lishi zhonglan* (Sixty years of Chinese architecture, 1949-2009: Historical compendium). Beijing: Zhongguo jianzhu gongye chubanshe, 2009.

______. *Zhongguo xiandai jianzhu ershijiang* (Twenty lectures on contemporary Chinese architecture). Shanghai: Shangwu yinshuguan, 2015.

______. *Zhongguo xiandai jianzhu shi* (History of contemporary Chinese architecture). Beijing: Zhongguo jianzhu gongye chubanshe, 2020.

Image Credits

Thirteen Factories, Guangzhou, 1757-1842
Fair Scholarly Use

Shopping Arcade, Haikou, Hainan, 1840s.
Keda Wang

Thomaz de Aquino, *Governor's Residence*, Macau, 1846-1849
Omitted

Hongcun, Huizhou, Anhui
Nancy Steinhardt

Father Nicholas Massa, *St. Francis Xavier Cathedral*, Dongjiadu (Dong Family Pier), Shanghai, 1849-1853 with later restoration
Keda Wang

Astor House, Shanghai, 1858 and later
Keda Wang

Dingling, Tomb of the Xianfeng emperor, Zunhua, Hebei, 1861
Keda Wang

Astor Hotel, Tianjin, 1864
Keda Wang

Chartered Bank of India, Australia, and China, Hankou, 1865
Keda Wang

Sir George Gilbert Scott and William Kidner, *Holy Trinity Church*, Shanghai, 1866-1869
Keda Wang

Wanghailou Church, Tianjin, 1869-1870
Keda Wang

Society for the Study of Chinese Architecture, Yibin, Sichuan, built 1862-1874; 1940-1946
Keda Wang

Hu Xueyuan Mansion, Hangzhou, 1872-1875
Keda Wang

Shi Family Mansion, Tianjin, 1875
Keda Wang

Yuantongbao Hall and *Gude Buddhist Monastery*, Hankou, 1877
Nancy Steinhardt

Post Office, Tianjin, 1878
Keda Wang

St. John's University, Shanghai, 1879
Keda Wang

Gabriel James Morrison, *Russell & Company Building*, Shanghai, 1881
Keda Wang

Jade Buddha Temple, Shanghai, 1882
Keda Wang

J. W. Hart, *Yangshupu Waterworks*, Shanghai, 1883
Keda Wang

Xiheying Church, Zhangjiakou, Hebei, 1887
Keda Wang

Church of The Savior, Beijing, 1890
Nancy Steinhardt

Gate of Supreme Harmony (Taihemen), Forbidden City, Beijing, 1894
Keda Wang

Summer Palace, Beijing, 1894
Yu Lina

Sheng Xuanhuai Residence, Shanghai, 1896
Keda Wang

Heinrich Becker and Richard Steel, *Russo-Chinese Bank*, Tianjin, 1896/1902
Keda Wang

Hengdaohezi Railway Park, Heilongjiang, 1897
Boxi Liu

V. V. Sakharov and others, *City Hall*, Dalian, 1900
Fair scholarly use

Sheshan Observatory, Shanghai, 1900
Keda Wang

F. H. Schmidt, Hamburg, *Imperial German Post Office*, Qingdao, 1900-1901
Keda Wang

Banque de l'Indo-Chine, Hankou, 1902
Keda Wang

Dongtang (East Church), Beijing, 1904
Anthony Clark

Wentrup, *Police Station and Court House*, Qingdao, 1904-1905
Keda Wang

W. Wutzler with site architect G. L. Hempel, *German Consulate*, Hankou, 1904-1905
Keda Wang

Korbinian Paugger, *Sacred Heart Cathedral*, Jinan, 1906
Keda Wang
Fair scholarly use

Qing Army and Naval Headquarters, Beijing, 1906
Keda Wang

Guangdong Guild Hall, Tianjin, 1907
Keda Wang

Saint Sophia Cathedral, Harbin, 1898-1907
Nancy Steinhardt

Mahike and Strasser, *German Governor's House*, Qingdao, 1904-1907
Keda Wang

Heinrich Becker and Carl Baedecker, *German-Asian Bank*, Jinan, 1907-1908
Keda Wang

Waterworks, Beijing, 1908
Keda Wang

Atkinson & Dallas, *Great Northern Telegraph Building Shanghai*, 1905-1908
Keda Wang

Huashan Hospital, Shanghai, 1907
Keda Wang

Walter Scott (1860-1917) and Carter, *Palace Hotel*, Shanghai, 1904-1909
Keda Wang

Lothar Marcks, *Bismarck Barracks*, Qingdao, 1900-1909
Keda Wang

Prayer Hall, Tianjin Great Mosque, Tianjin, 1909
Nancy Steinhardt

Yokohama Specie Bank, Dalian, 1909
Keda Wang

Curt Rothkegel, *Christian Church*, Qingdao, 1908-1910
Keda Wang

H. Tarrant and George Christopher Wingrove/ Moorhead and Halse, *Shanghai Club*, Bund, Shanghai, 1910
Keda Wang

Beijing Zoo Entrance, Beijing, 1910
Keda Wang

Bower of the Spirit Pool, Forbidden City, Beijing, 1909-1911
Jianwei Zhang

Aston Webb and Ingress Bell, *Supreme Court Building*, Hong Kong, 1903-1912
Fair scholarly use

Lüshun Museum, Lüshun, 1915
Nancy Steinhardt

St. Joseph's Cathedral and Catholic Mission, Tianjin, 1913-1916
Keda Wang

James R. Edmunds, Jr., *Swasey Hall*, Lingnan University, Guangzhou, 1917
Keda Wang

Mausoleum of Yuan Shikai, Anyang, 1916-1918
Keda Wang

Henry Murphy and Richard Dana, *Auditorium, Tsinghua College*, Beijing, 1920
iStock.com

Atkinson & Dallas Architects and Engineers, *Kailuan Mining Administration Building*, Tianjin, 1919-1921
Keda Wang

Shattuck & Hussey, *Peking Union Medical College*, Beijing, 1921
Keda Wang

Tug Wilson, *HSBC (Hong Kong and Shanghai Banking Corporation) Building*, The Bund, Shanghai, 1921-1923
Keda Wang and Wen Sen Tan (iStock.com)

László Hudec, *The Normandie*, Shanghai, 1924
N502FZWikimeida

Sun Zhixia (1882-1975), *Nantong*, Jiangsu, 1911-1926
Keda Wang

Charles Gonda (1889-1969), *Sun Sun Department Store*, Shanghai, 1926
Keda Wang

Shen Liyuan, *Salt Industry Bank*, Tianjin, 1926
Keda Wang

Palmer & Turner, *Customs House*, Shanghai, 1925-1927
Keda Wang

Paul Müller, *Quanyechang*, Tianjin, 1927
Keda Wang

László Hudec, *Huadong Hospital*, Shanghai, 1926
Keda Wang

Palmer & Turner, *Sassoon House* (Cathay Hotel), 1926-1929
Robert Deutscher (Wikipedia)

Liu Jipiao, *West Lake Exposition*, Hangzhou, 1929
Keda Wang

Arcade, Quanzhou, 1930s
Huitu.com/Good bird Yu Yuan

László Hudec, *China Baptist Publication Building*, Shanghai, 1930
Keda Wang and Nancy Steinhardt

Nankai High School, Tianjin, 1906-1931
Keda Wang

Lü Yanzhi and Zhao Shen, *Sun Yat-Sen Mausoleum*, Nanjing, 1929-1931
Keda Wang

Lü Yanzhi, *Sun Yat-Sen Memorial Hall*, Guangzhou, 1929-1931
Nancy Steinhardt

Kwan (Guan) Songsheng, Chu Pin (Zhu Bin), and Yang Tingbao, *National Stadium*, Nanjing, 1931
Nancy Steinhardt

Cheefoo Club, Yantai, Shandong, 1931
Keda Wang

Trinity Catholic Church, Dali, Yunnan, 1931
Wikipedia

Poy Gum Lee (Li Jinpei) (1900-1968), Robert (Wenzhao) Fan, and Zhao Shen, *YMCA*, Shanghai, 1931
Keda Wang

Palmer & Turner, *Grosvenor House*, Shanghai, 1932
Keda Wang

Charles Gonda, *Cathay Theater*, Shanghai, 1932
Keda Wang

Yang Tingbao (1901-1982), *Musical Stage*, Purple Mountains, Nanjing, 1932-1933
Nancy Steinhardt

Charles Henry Stableford (1863-1944) and Arthur Carr Wheeler, *Shanghai Municipal Council Abbatoir*, Shanghai, 1933
Keda Wang

Spence Robinson and Partners, *Race Club*, Shanghai, 1933
Keda Wang

Liu Shiying, *Wang Boqun Residence*, Shanghai, 1930-1934
Keda Wang

László Hudec, *Park Hotel*, Shanghai, 1931-1934
Wikimedia

Yang Ximiao, *Paramount Ballroom*, Shanghai, 1933-1934
Bogdan Lazar (iStock.com)

Palmer & Turner, *Metropole Hotel*, Shanghai, 1934
Keda Wang

Veysseyre & Kruze, *Gascogne Apartments*, Shanghai, 1934
Keda Wang

Zhuang Jun, *Shanghai Mint*, Shanghai, 1921-1930
Keda Wang

Yang Tingbao, *Dahua Cinema*, Nanjing, 1935
Keda Wang

Dong Dayou, *China Aviation Association Building*, Shanghai, 1935
Keda Wang

Endo Arata, *Central Bank*, Changchun, Jilin, 1934-1935
Keda Wang

Aiga Kensuka, *Ministry of Justice* and Ishii Tatsurō, *State Council Building*, Changchun, 1935 and 1936
Keda Wang and iStock.com David Eric

Luke Him Sau (Liu Qianshou) and Palmer & Turner, *Bank of China*, Shanghai, 1936
Keda Wang

Hunke and Müller, *Bohai Building*, Tianjin, 1936
VGC.com: VCG211305153720

Allied Architects, *Moller Villa*, Shanghai, 1936
Karl Johaentges (Alamy)

F. H. Kales, *Wuhan University*, Hubei, 1937
Howchoue (Wikimedia)

Percy Tilley, *Liza Hardoon Building*, Shanghai, 1938
Keda Wang

Makino Masami, *Supreme Court*, Changchun, Jilin, 1938
Keda Wang

László Hudec, *D. V. Woo's Residence*, Shanghai, after 1938
Keda Wang

Jinmu Hall, Changchun, 1940
Keda Wang

Robert Fan, *Majestic Theater (Meiqi)*, Nanjing, 1941
Keda Wang

Shang Qixu, *Nanyue Martyrs' Shrine*, Hengyang, Hunan, 1942
Keda Wang

Zhuan Xueren, *Ma Bufang Mansion*, Xining, Qinghai, 1942-1943 and *Ma Buqing Mansion*, Linxia, Gansu, 1938-1945
Keda Wang

Fred Rowntree, *West China Hospital, Sichuan University*, Chengdu, Sichuan, 1946
Phillip Lejeanvre (Alamy)

Tong Jun, *Apartments for Americans*, Blocks A and B, Nanjing, 1947
Keda Wang

Liang Sicheng, advisor; Xu Jingzhi, Li Huibo, and others, *National Central Museum*, Nanjing, 1948
Farm (Wikimedia) and Keda Wang

Yang Tingbao, *Sun Ke Villa*, Nanjing, 1948
Keda Wang

Liu Shiying, *Library and Grand Auditorium*, Hunan University, Changsha, 1951
Keda Wang

Yang Tingbao and Yang Kuanglin, *Peace Hotel*, Beijing, 1951-1953
Keda Wang

Wang Dingzheng, *Caoyang Xincun*, Shanghai, 1951-1953
Keda Wang

Hong Qing, *People's Grand Hotel*, Xi'an, 1951-1953
Keda Wang

Wang Fuchen, *Palace of Geology*, Changchun, Jilin, 1953
Keda Wang

FAW (First Automobile Works) (Changchun YIQI [Changchun First Car]) Factory), Changchun, Jilin, 1953
Fair scholarly use

Beijing University Foreign Housing, Beijing, 1952-1954
Keda Wang

Xu Zhong (1912-1985), *Aoyuan*, Jimei Educational Village, Xiamen, Fujian, 1950-1954
Keda Wang

Huang Yulin and Ha Xiongwen, *Wenyuan Hall*, Tongji University, Shanghai, 1953-1954
Keda Wang

Dai Nianci (1920-1991), *West Building, Beijing Hotel*, Beijing, 1954
Keda Wang

Zhang Bo, *Friendship Hotel*, Beijing, 1954
Keda Wang

Lin Leyi, *Capital Theater*, Beijing, 1954-1955
Keda Wang

Zhang Kaiji, *Sanlihe Government Complex*, Beijing, 1952-1955
Chang Yung Ho

Baiwanzhuang Residential Area, Beijing, 1953-1956
Keda Wang

Viktor Andreyev, Benjamin Chen, and others, *Sino-Soviet Friendship Hall*, Shanghai, 1954-1955
Wikipedia and Alamy

Lin Leyi and Zhang Zhaoping, *Telegraph Service Building*, Beijing, 1955-1957
Keda Wang

Yan Xinghua, *Central Broadcasting Building*, Beijing, 1957
TAO Images (Alamy)

Zhang Kaiji and Song Rong, Architecture Design and Research Institute, *Beijing Planetarium*, Building A, Beijing, 1957
Keda Wang

Liang Sicheng, *Monument to the People's Heroes*, Beijing, 1949-1958
Keda Wang

Zhao Dongri, Shen Qi, Zhang Bo, and others, *Great Hall of the People*, Beijing, 1958-1959
iStock

Zhang Bo, Sun Peiyao, and others of Beijing Institute of Architectural Design, *Minorities Cultural Palace*, Beijing, 1958-1959
Keda Wang

Beijing Institute of Architectural Design, *Workers' Stadium*, Beijing, 1959
Keda Wang

Yang Tingbao and Chen Deng'ao, *Beijing Railway Station*, Beijing, 1959
Keda Wang

Dai Nianci and others of Beijing Institute of Architectural Design, *National Art Museum*, Beijing, 1958-1962
Annie Budou (Huitu.com)

Dai Fudong, *Meiling (Plum Retreat)*, East Lake, Wuhan, 1958-1963
Kyra Xinwei Yao and Wikipedia

Mo Bozhi (1915-2003) and Zheng Zuliang, *Shuangxi Villas*, Guangzhou, 1962-1965
Keda Wang

Zhang Bo and others, Beijing Institute of Architectural Design, *Qijiayuan Diplomatic Residential Apartments*, Beijing, 1973-1975
Keda Wang

Shanghai People's Institute of Architectural Design, *Shanghai Indoor Stadium*, Shanghai, 1975
Feifeigang/Stock

Xu Mengpei, Yang Tingbao, and others, *Memorial Hall of Chairman Mao*, Tian'anmen Square, Beijing, 1976-1977
iStock.com

I.M. Pei, *Fragrant Hill Hotel*, Beijing, 1981
WikiCommons

Beijing Institute of Architectural Design, *Liulichang*, Beijing, 1980s
Keda Wang

Beckett International, *Great Wall Hotel*, Beijing, 1983
Keda Wang and Huitu.com

Qi Kang, *Wuyi Mountain Villa*, Mount Wuyi, Fujian, 1983
Keda Wang

Xiang Xinran (1940-2021), *Yellow Crane Tower*, Snake Hill, Wuhan, Hubei, 1981-1985
Keda Wang

Dai Nianci and Fu Xiurong, *Queli Guest House*, Qufu, Shandong, 1985
Keda Wang

Chen Jihong (1915-2009), *Square Pagoda Garden*, Songjiang, Shanghai, 1986
Nancy Steinhardt

Qi Kang, *Meiyuan Xinchun Memorial*, Nanjing, 1987
Keda Wang

Huqingyutang Museum of Traditonal Chinese Medicine, Hangzhou, 1988
Keda Wang

Lu Jiwei, *Kempinski Hotel*, Beijing, 1992
Keda Wang

Jia Huan Cheng, Zhang Xiulin, and Lin Benlin; Shanghai Construction Group, *Oriental Pearl Radio and Television Tower*, Shanghai, 1991-1994
Wikicommons

Xing Tonghe, *Shanghai Museum*, Shanghai, 1996
iStock.com and Edwin Remsburg (Alamy)

Liu Li, *Henderson (Hengji) Center*, Beijing, 1996
Keda Wang

Qi Kang, *Henan Museum*, Zhengzhou, Henan, 1997
Gary Todd (Wikimedia)

Arte Charpentier, *Shanghai Grand Theater*, Shanghai, 1998
iStock.com

Skidmore, Owings & Merrill, *Jin Mao Tower*, Shanghai, 1994-1999
iStock

Pei Architects, *Bank of China Headquarters*, Beijing, 1999
Keda Wang

Wang Shu, Lu Wenyu, and Tong Ming, *Wenzheng College Library*, Suzhou University, Suzhou, 1998-2000
Keda Wang

Zhang Lei, AZL Architects, *Nanjing University Graduate Student Dormitory*, Nanjing, 2000
Zhang Lei

Foster and Partners, *Jiushi Headquarters*, Pudong, Shanghai, 1995-2001
Keda Wang

Twelve Architects, *Commune by the Wall*, Beijing, 2002
Keda Wang

John Portman, *Tomorrow Square*, Shanghai, 1996-2003
Keda Wang

Wang Lu, *Tiantai Museum*, Tiantai, Zhejiang, 1999-2003
Wang Lu

Ma Qingyun, MADA spam, *Father's House*, Lantian, Xi'an, Shaanxi, 2003
Repco and Alamy

Chang Yung Ho, *Hebei Educational Publishing House*, Shijiazhuang, Hebei, 2000-2003
Courtesy of Chang Yung He and photo by Shu He

GMP, *Nanning International Conference and Exhibition Center*, Nanning, Guangxi, 1999-2005
GMP

Kohn Pedersen Fox, *China Natural Offshore Oil Corpotation Headquarters*, Beijing, 2002-2006
KPF

Zhu Pei and Wu Tong, *Blur Hotel*, Beijing, 2004-2006
Zhu Pei and Wu Tong

Wang Shu and Lu Wenyu, *Ceramic House*, Jinhua, Zhejiang, 2003-2006
Keda Wang

I. M. Pei, *Suzhou Museum*, Suzhou, 2006
Istock
Nancy Steinhardt

Paul Andreu, *Centre for the Performing Arts*, Beijing, 2007
Alamy and Wikipedia

Herzog & de Meuron, *National Stadium* (Bird's Nest), Beijing, 2007
Alamy and Wikipedia

Arata Isozaki, *Central Academy Of Fine Arts*, Beijing, 2008
Alamy

Kohn Pedersen Fox, *World Financial Center*, Shanghai, 1997-2008
KPF

Wang Shu, *Ningbo Museum*, Ningbo, 2008
Keda Wang

Steven Holl, *Linked Hybrid*, Beijing, 2005-2009
Steven Holl and Keda Wang

Henn Architekten, *Beijing International Automotive Exposition Center*, Beijing, 2009
Keda Wang

Guangdong Maritime Silk Road Museum, Hailing Island, Yangjiang, Guangdong, 2004-2009
Keda Wang

Information Based Architecture, *Canton Tower*, Guangzhou, 2009
Pixaby

Hassell, *Alibaba Headquarters*, Hangzhou, 2009
China Images

Ge Xiurun, *Baiheliang Underwater Museum*, Chongqing, 2009
Keda Wang

Rocco Design Architects, *Guangdong Museum*, Guangzhou, 2010
Rocco Design

Zaha Hadid, *Opera House*, Guangzhou, 2005-2010
Zaha Hadid (office)

He Jingtang, *China Pavilion*, Shanghai, 2010,
iStock.com

Architectural Design and Research Institute, Tsinghua University, *Century Hall*, Tsinghua University, Beijing, 2010
Keda Wang

AUBE, *Guiyang Conference and Exhibition Center*, Guiyang, 2011
Alamy

Hiroshi Oshima, *Concert Hall*, Xuzhou, 2011
Stock.adobe.com

Kengo Kuma & Associates, *Zhi Museum*, Xinjin, Sichuan, 2011
Keda Wang

Sun Wei, HWCD Associates, *Bamboo Courtyard Teahouse*, Yangzhou, 2012
Keda Wang

Rem Koolhaas, *CCTV Tower*, Beijing, 2012
Wikipedia and iStock

Tianjin University Research Institute of Architectural Design & Urban Planning, *Liuzhou Fantastic Stones Museum*, Liuzhou, Guangxi, 2012
Zhang Hua

Zaha Hadid Architects, *Galaxy Soho Building*, Beijing, 2012
Alamy

Chang Yung Ho, *Vertical Glass House*, Shanghai, 2013
Courtesy of Chang Yung Ho and photo by Lyu Hengzhong

Steven Holl, *Nanjing Sifang Museum of Art and Architecture*, Nanjing, 2003-2013
Steven Holl and Keda Wang

Li Xinggang, *Jixi Museum*, Jixi, Anhui, 2013
Xia Zhi

Value Factory, Shenzhen, 2013
Nansha Original Design

JDP Architects, *Guangzhou Circle*, Guangzhou, 2013
iStock

MAD, *China Wood Sculpture Museum*, Harbin, 2013
Keda Wang

New Century Global Mall, Chengdu, 2013
Keda Wang

Paul Andreu, *Jinan Grand Theater*, Jinan, Shangdong, 2013
Keda Wang

Isozaki Arata, *Himalayas Art Museum*, Shanghai, 2013
Keda Wang

Liu Yichun, Atelier Deschaus, *Long Museum*, West Bund, Shanghai, 2012
Keda Wang

Stufish Entertainment Architects, *Han Show Theater*, Wuhan, 2014
Keda Wang

Dong Yugan, *Red Brick Art Museum*, Beijing, 2014
Keda Wang

Zhang Lei, *AZL*, *Wanjing Garden Chapel*, Nanjing, 2014
Keda Wang

Gensler, *Shanghai Tower*, Shanghai, 2015
Shanghai Business Operation and iStock

Ma Yansong, MAD Architects, *Opera House*, Harbin, Heilongjiang, 2015
Wikipedia and Alamy

Chen Wei, *Bao'en Monastery Pagoda*, Nanjing, 2015
Courtesy of Chen Wei; photograph by Xiangyun Studio

Von Gerkan & Partners, *Guanghualu Soho 2*, Beijing, 2015
Keda Wang

Coop Himmelb(l)au, *Museum of Contemporary Art and Planning Exhibition*, Shenzhen, 2015
Keda Wang

THAD, *Tsinghua University Library*, Phase Four, Beijing, 2016
Keda Wang

Kohn Pedersen Fox, *Ping an Finance Center*, Shenzhen, 2017
KPF and iStock

Neri & Hu, *Tsingpu Retreat*, Yangzhou, 2017
iStock

Ma Yansong, MAD Architects, *Chaoyang Park Plaza*, Beijing, 2017
MAD

NBBJ, *Tencent Seafront Towers*, Shenzhen, 2018
iStock

Zaha Hadid, *Leeza Soho*, Beijing, 2019
Hadid Associates; photo by Hufton+Crow

Kohn Pedersen Fox, *Citic Tower* (China Zun), Beijing, 2019
KPF

Wang Shu, *Lin'an Museum*, Hangzhou, 2020
Keda Wang

Foster and Partners, *Datong Art Museum*, Datong, 2021
Keda Wang

Kohn Pedersen Fox, *Huamu* Lot 10, Shanghai, 2022
KPF

Beijing Municipal Institute of City Planning & Design, and CCTN Architect Design Company, *Shougang Industrial Heritage Park*, Shijingshan, Beijing, 1919-2005; 2008-2022
Keda Wang

Cover image by Hu Chen from Unsplash